RANGER HANDBOOK

THE UNITED STATES ARMY
INFANTRY SCHOLL FOR BENNING,
GEORGIA

Fredonia Books
Amsterdam, The Netherlands

Ranger Handbook

by
United States Army Infantry School
Fort Benning, Georgia

ISBN: 1-58963-797-6

Reprinted from the 1970 edition

Fredonia Books
Amsterdam, The Netherlands
http://www.fredoniabooks.com

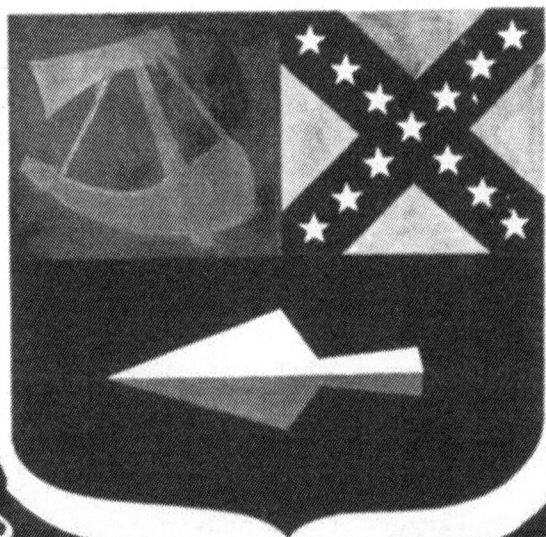

RANGERS·LEAD THE WAY

RANGER BADGE

The badge, or coat or arms, consists of four portions: the lion in the crest and three sections in the shield. Each of these portions represents service from the 17th through 20th Centuries.

Crest: This is composed of a lion passant quadrant, color gold surrounded by a wreath, colors green and red. The lion alludes to honorable service to the British Crown prior to the American Revolution. Wreath is in colors of French Fourragere which was awarded to two battalions during World War II. The traditional heraldic rope or link is colored white, the old color of American Infantry, and Army Blue.

Shield: The shield is divided into three unequal portions Left top portion represents service in 18th Century with background of forest green to indicate the early Rangers' knowledge of woodlore. Tomahawk and powder horn explain their application with light infantry and scouting learned from the American Indians. Right top portion is Confederate battle-flag which refers to distinguished service to the Confederacy during War between the States. Lower portion, larger than top sections, indicates increased service during 20th Century. The spearhead represents a nickname first given to World War II Rangers and later carried on in Korea - "The Spearheaders." Black background alludes to the night foul weather and rough country - the setting for many successful Ranger operations. Colors black and gold designate present Ranger Tab awarded to Ranger trained officers and NCO's. Entire shield is framed in contemporary Infantry color, azure, to symbolize that we are of the Infantry. Scroll underneath shield refers to original insignia worn by Rangers of battalions in World War II and companies in Korea. This insignia was patterned after the British Commando patch and indicates our attachment to this unit who was responsible for training Rangers initially in 1942. The motto, "Rangers, Lead the Way" originated on D-Day in 1944 during the fierce fighting at "Omaha Beach."

FOREWORD

This handbook has been compiled for the use of the Ranger student and graduate. The material within has been extracted from lesson plans and field manuals applicable to the Ranger POI. This material has been organized into three sections.

Section I - Checklists and Formats - For use by the experienced students; ones who have assimilated the background information contained in Section II.

Section II - Reference Material - For ready reference to major subjects taught in the Ranger Course.

Section III - Training Notes - Diagrams of Ranger training areas for reference once the Ranger graduate has returned to his parent unit.

INDEX

CHAPTER ONE

WARNING ORDER

The patrol warning order consists of the following:
- A. A brief statement of the situation.
- B. Mission of the patrol.
- C. General instructions:
    1. General and special organization.
    2. Uniform and equipment common to all.
    3. Weapons, ammunition, and equipment.
    4. Chain of command.
    5. A time schedule for the patrol's guidance.
    6. Time, place, uniform and equipment for receiving the patrol order.
    7. Times and places for inspections and rehearsals.
- D. Specific instructions:
    1. To subordinate leaders.
    2. To special purpose teams or key individuals

TROOP LEADING STEPS

1. Begin planning.
    a. Plan use of time.
    b. Analyze terrain and situation.
    c. Make preliminary plan.
    d. Issue warning order.
2. Coordinate (continuous throughout).
3. Make reconnaissance.
4. Complete detailed plan.
5. Issue operations order.
6. Supervise (inspection, rehearsals, execution).

APL CHECKLIST

During the conduct of a patrol the assistant patrol leader's function is similar to that of the platoon sergeants the following checklist outlines the normal duties the APL is expected to perform.

1. ACTIONS IN A PATROL BASE.
    a. Assist in the occupation of the patrol base.
    b. Assists in supervising the establishment and adjustment of the perimeter.
    c. Dispatches R/S teams and establishes OP's.
    d. Maintains security in the patrol base.
        (1) Keep movement and noise to a minimum.
        (2) Supervise camouflage and perimeter preparation.
        (3) Periodically inspect the perimeter and insure sectors of fire are assigned.
        (4) Insure that designated personnel remain alert, and that equipment is maintained in a state of readiness.
    e. Requisitions supplies, water, ammo and supervises their redistribution.
    f. Supervise the priority of work and insure its accomplishment.
        (1) Maintenance plan.
        (2) Hygiene plan.
        (3) Messing plan.
        (4) Water plan.
        (5) Rest plan.
    g. Perform additional tasks assigned by the patrol leader and assist the patrol leader in every way possible.

2. ACTIONS DURING MOVEMENT AND AT HALTS.
    a. Take necessary actions to facilitate movement.
    b. Insure patrol members remain alert at all
times.
    c. Supervise rear security during movement.
    d. Supervise the establishment and maintenance
of security at halts.
    e. Maintain noise, camouflage and light discipline
    f. Perform additional tasks as required by the
patrol leader and assist the patrol leader in every way
possible.

3. ACTIONS IN THE OBJECTIVE AREA.
    a. Assist in the occupation of the ORP.
    b. Supervise the establishment and maintenance
of an alert system in the ORP.
    c. Supervise the maintenance of weapons and
equipment in the ORP.
    d. Accompany the patrol leader on reconnaissance
as required.
    e. Maintain control and security during movement
to and deployment in the ORP.
    f. Assist the patrol leader in control.
    g. Supervise reorganization and redistribution of
ammunition and equipment.
    h. Perform additional tasks assigned by the patrol
leader and assist the patrol leader in every way possible.

CHAPTER TWO

COORDINATION

1. AIR MOVEMENT AND RESUPPLY.
   a. Enemy and Friendly Situation.
      (1) Indications of enemy locations in the zone of operations.
      (2) Location and axis of friendly movements.
   b. Patrol mission.
   c. Number and type aircraft available and support desired:
      (1) Fixed or rotary-wing aircraft.
      (2) Equipment resupply or air movement.
   d. Weather information.
   e. Availability of aircraft for rehearsal of loading and unloading procedure.
   f. Location and time of pickup and landing.
   g. Manifesting procedures and responsibilities.
   h. Flight route, location of checkpoints, communication checkpoints, obstacles and use of diversionary landings to deceive the enemy.
   i. Flight information, altitude and prelanding warning to alert personnel.
   j. Call signs, frequencies, and alternate visual means of communications.

2. FORWARD UNIT.
   a. Identify yourself and your unit.
   b. Size of patrol.
   c. Time and place of departure and return (location of GAP).
   d. General area of operations.
   e. Information on terrain and vegetation.
   f. Known or suspected enemy positions and obstacles.
   g. Possible enemy ambush sites.
   h. Knowledge of latest enemy activity.

2.01

     i.   Detailed information on friendly positions.

     j.   Coordinate fire and barrier plan.

     k.   location of initial rallying point and assembly area if applicable.

     l.   Support unit can furnish.

         (1) Fire support.

         (2) Litter teams.

         (3) Navigational signals or aids.

         (4) Guides.

         (5) Communication plan between the patrol and the forward unit.

         (6) Reaction squads.

         (7) Other.

     m. Exchange call signs and frequencies.

     n. Exchange of pyrotechnic plans.

     o. Confirm challenge and password.

     p. Information passed on to relieving unit.

     q. Emergency signals and codewords.

3. FIRE SUPPORT COORDINATION.

     a. Mission.

  *b. Route (include alternate route of return).

  *c. Target list (include danger areas).

     d. Ammunition and fuzes available.

     e. Location of units to fire.

  *f. Registration points and time of registration (if applicable).

     g. Communications information (to include primary and alternate means, and emergency signals).

     h. Control measures.

         (1) Checkpoints.

         (2) Phase lines.

         (3) Fire coordination lines.

         (4) No fire lines.

         (5) Time of departure and return.

     i. Availability of:

         (1) Aerial observer.

         (2) Forward observers.

        j.   Enemy information available from artillery
sources:
  Also included on fire support overlay (See Chap 8).

CHAPTER THREE

OPERATIONS ORDER FOR A PATROL

1. SITUATION.
    a. Enemy.
        (1) Weather.
        (2) Terrain.
        (3) Identification.
        (4) Location.
        (5) Activity.
        (6) Strength.
    b. Friendly.
        (1) Mission of next higher unit.
        (2) Location and planned actions of neighboring units.
        (3) Fire support available.
        (4) Missions and routes of other patrols.
    c. Attachments and Detachments:

2. MISSION

3. EXECUTION
    a. Concept of Operation - the overall plan - and missions of elements, teams, and individuals in the objective
    b. Other missions, not in the objective area, for elements, teams and individuals. Included are such tasks as navigation, security during movement, and security at halts.
    c. Coordinating Instructions.
        (1) Time of departure and return.
        (2) Formations and order of movement.
        (3) Route and alternate routes.
        (4) Departure from and reentry of friendly areas.
        (5) Rallying points and actions at rallying points.
        (6) Actions on enemy contact.
        (7) Actions at danger areas.
        (8) Actions at objective.
        (9) Fire support
        (10) Rehearsals and inspections.
        (11) Debriefing.

(12) Other actions.

4. ADMINISTRATION AND LOGISTICS.
   a. Rations.
   b. Arms and ammunition.
   c. Uniform and equipment.
   d. Method of handling wounded and prisoners.

5. COMMAND AND SIGNAL.
   a. Signal.
      (1) Signals to be used within patrol.
      (2) Communications with higher headquarters.
         (a) Radio call sign.
         (b) Primary and alternate frequencies.
         (c) Reports.
         (d) Codes.
      (3) Challenge and password.
   b. Command.
      (1) Chain of command.
      (2) Location of patrol leader and assistant patrol
leader in formation.

Patrol annexes may be necessary to make the plan
more complete. Also, certain information may be extracted from the operations order and issued as an
annex to promote clarity and understanding. Information
that may be issued in annex form include the aerial resupply plan, the fire support plan, the patrol base plan and the
air movement plan.

The operations order annex follows the normal five
paragraph format. Certain of these paragraphs may be
omitted if they have been covered thoroughly in the operations order, or if they do not contain information that
specifically applies to the annex mission.

3.02

PLANNING IN THE FIELD

In most respects planning in the field is the same as planning in base camp. The following items are presented in their most logical sequence to assist the leader faced with planning for an operation in the field.

1. Time Schedule - Normally all missions include a time by which the mission must be accomplished. It is therefore essential that the leader plan the efficient use of available time. Backward planning steps are necessary before a warning order can be issued.

2. Warning Order - A warning order is essential so that personnel may begin preparing for the mission. (See Chap 1 for format.)

3. Planning - Plan for the actual mission accomplish. ment (i.e.; actions at the objective) first. Then fill in the remainder of the order with the necessary control measures, coordinating instructions and details which will support the actions at the objective.

4. Operations Order for A Patrol - Time permitting every item in a normal order should be covered. As a minimum, however, the order should include the current situation, mission, concept, missions of subordinate elements, teams and individuals, routes to and from the objective, actions at the objective, command and signal and any other changes from the original order.

5. Rehearsals - Time permitting a brief rehearsal should be conducted. A "talk-through" is better than no rehearsal at all. During a rehearsal in the field security must be maintained at all times.

3.03

6. Inspections - As a minimum all weapons, ammo distribution, radios and special equipment essential to mission accomplishment should be inspected prior to departure from the patrol base.

CHAPTER FOUR

EXAMPLE OF AN OPERATIONS ORDER
FOR AN AMBUSH PATROL

1. SITUATION
   a. Enemy Forces: Numbers, order of march, dress, weapons. Any VIP's -- where located; habits of party concerned. Terrain: Use of maps, air photos, local knowledge, guides. Weather conditions. Unfriendly civilians, their locations and habits.
   b. Friendly Forces: Mission of next higher unit and other units of operational concern; guides or surrendered enemy to accompany; clearance with other units; supporting units; friendly civilians.
   c. Attachments and Detachments:

2. MISSION

3. EXECUTION
   a. Concept of Operation - the overall plan - and missions of elements, teams, and individuals in the ambush site.
   b. Other missions, not in the ambush site, for elements, teams and individuals. Included are such tasks as navigation, security during movement, and security at halts.
   c. Coordinating Instructions.
      (1) Time of departure and return.
      (2) Formation and order of movement.
      (3) Departure from and reentry of friendly areas.
      (4) Routes to and from ambush site.
      (5) Actions at danger areas.
      (6) Actions on enemy contact.
      (7) Rallying points and actions at rallying points.
      (8) Actions at objective:
          (a) Organization of ambush site: positions and sectors of fire; location of early warning security; killing zone; use of mines, booby traps, and grenades to block

avenues of escape; provision for all-round security of patrol in ambush site.

(b) Movement into ambush positions: ORP, reconnaissance, release point, routes of elements into positions, preparation and camouflage of positions.

(c) Actions in ambush site: Measures to insure patrol is alert; noise and light discipline; signals to call off ambush, open fire, cease fire, assault, pursue, alert members to enemy approach; plan for closing with enemy, searching, etc.; withdrawal plan; deception plan.

(9) Rehearsals and inspections: men with colds? ammo and magazines properly prepared? weapons zeroed? knowledge of plan?

(10) Fire support.

(11) Debriefing.

(12) Other actions.

4. ADMINISTRATION AND LOGISTICS

a. Rations.

b. Weapons, grenades, mines, booby traps, ammunition; equipment for communications, night illumination.

c. Uniform and equipment, camouflage, footgear for moving into position.

d. Transportation to and from area.

e. Medical: patrol aid man, evacuation plan, plan for treatment and evacuation of wounded enemy.

f. Relief plan and admin area (for long-term ambushes).

5. COMMAND AND SIGNAL

a. Signal.

(1) Signals within patrol.

(2) Communications with headquarters - frequencies, codes, runners, success signal; signals for air support, fire support, other support.

(3) Challenge and password; other identification.

b. Command.

(1) Chain of command.

(2) Location of PL and APL during all stages of operation.

NOTE: The foregoing operations order for an ambush operation is provided as a planning guide. For any specific ambush operation, some of the items listed will probably be non-applicable and will have to be omitted, while other items of special concern for the operation will have to be added. Note also how the various considerations for an ambush operation are organized using the standard 5-paragraph format; the same method should be used to organize a detailed plan for any other type of patrol operation.

CHAPTER FIVE

DEBRIEFING
(Patrol Report)

TO:

MAPS
   A. Size and composition of patrol.
   B. Mission.
   C. Time of departure.
   D. Time of return.
   E. Routes.
   F. Terrain (out and back).
   G. Any map corrections.
   H. Enemy.
   I. Results of encounter with the enemy.
   J. Miscellaneous information.
   K. Condition of patrol.
   L. Conclusions and recommendations.

Signature, Rank, and Organization of Patrol Leader.

   M. Additional remarks by interrogator.

Signature, Rank, Organization of Debriefer. Date of De briefing.

CHAPTER SIX

ACTIONS AT THE OBJECTIVE

1. General: Although actions at the objective will vary due to different missions, terrain, and enemy and friendly situations, certain activities are normally performed in sequence for all patrol missions. These activities include halting prior to reaching the objective area, conducting a leader's recon, withdrawing from the objective rallying point (ORP), and dissemination of information gathered on the objective to all patrol members.

    a. Halt prior to reaching the objective area. This position may be the location of the tentative ORP. The position of the tentative ORP should be reconned by a small team to insure that it is suitable, prior to occupation by the entire patrol.

    b. The leader's recon is conducted to pinpoint the objective, and to confirm the plan.

    (1) During the leader's recon, the patrol leader may find that changes have to be made to the original plan. These changes are issued to all patrol members in a frag order.

    (2) The steps for making a leader's recon are:

    (a) Issue a contingency plan to cover actions to be taken in the event you fail to return.

    (b) Take the necessary subordinate leaders if appropriate.

    (c) Select a release point if necessary for additional control.

    (d) Confirm the withdrawal plan, to include confirming the location of the objective rallying point.

    (e) Maintain communications between the patrol leader and the patrol.

    (f) Maintain surveillance of the objective once the leader's recon has been accomplished.

(g) Use maximum stealth.

(h) Issue a frag order upon return.

c. Withdrawal from objective area to the ORP.

(1) The ORP is a rallying point near the objective where the patrol reassembles after the mission is accomplished. (Where appropriate, this can be used as the point from which the leader's recon is conducted and from which elements and teams move into position to accomplish the mission.)

(2) The characteristics of an ORP are: affords concealment, easy to defend for a short period of time, away from natural lines of drift, and easy enough to locate so that the patrol can be quickly and stealthily reassembled after the action.

(3) During the planning of the patrol, a tentative ORP is selected based on a map recon or, if possible, a physical recon.

(4) During reorganization, a chain of command is reestablished, a quick status report to include ammo and equipment is rendered by the element and team leaders, and a frag order is issued based on the patrol's overall capabilities.

d. Information gathered on the objective must be disseminated to each member of the patrol to insure that the information has the best possible chance of getting back. It may not be tactically sound to disseminate information in the ORP. However, do it as soon as possible.

2. The Reconnaissance Patrol.

a. Typical methods of organization:

(1) If the objective to be reconnoitered is restricted in area and clearly defined so that security elements are expected to perform their function from one fixed location (as in most point reconnaissance missions):

6. 02

```
                    ┌─────────┐
                    │ PTL HQS │
                    └────┬────┘
         ┌───────────────┴───────────────┐
    ┌─────────┐                      ┌─────────┐
    │  RECON  │                      │ SEC'Y   │
    │  ELEM   │                      │  ELEM   │
    └────┬────┘                      └────┬────┘
   ┌─────┼─────┐                 ┌────────┼────────┐
┌───────┐┌───────┐┌───────┐  ┌────────┐┌────────┐┌────────┐
│RCN TM ││RCN TM ││RCN TM │  │SEC'Y TM││SEC'Y TM││SEC'Y TM│
└───────┘└───────┘└───────┘  └────────┘└────────┘└────────┘
```

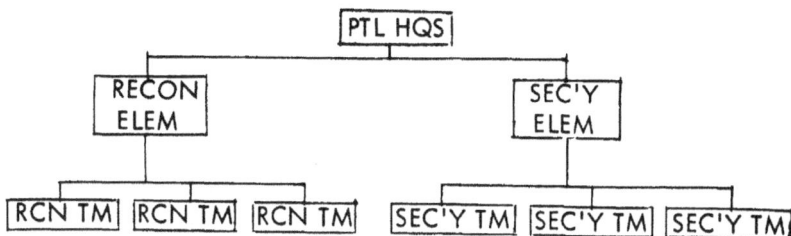

(2) If the objective to be reconnoitered is not clearly defined and located, so that movement into or through the objective area by mutually supported bounds is expected to be necessary (as in most area reconnaissance missions):

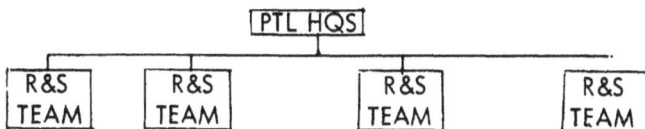

```
                    ┌─────────┐
                    │ PTL HQS │
                    └────┬────┘
   ┌────────┬───────────┴──┬──────────────────┐
┌──────┐ ┌──────┐      ┌──────┐          ┌──────┐
│ R&S  │ │ R&S  │      │ R&S  │          │ R&S  │
│ TEAM │ │ TEAM │      │ TEAM │          │ TEAM │
└──────┘ └──────┘      └──────┘          └──────┘
```

(3) In a small reconnaissance patrol, patrol headquarters may form a part of the recon element or of one R&S team, rather than being a separate element. The number and strength of recon teams, security teams, R&S teams, etc., must be determined according to the patrol strength, the mission, and the terrain.

b. Techniques for conducting reconnaissance patrols.

(1) All members of a patrol, regardless of their specific mission, must be alert to observe any information of the enemy or terrain, and to record it by notes or sketches when necessary.

(2) Maximum stealth, patience, and a well-rehearsed plan are the secrets of success.

6.03

(3) Battlefield noises can often be used to cover the sounds of movement made by a patrol in close proximity to the enemy.

(4) Binoculars are an invaluable aid to reconnaissance, both day and night.

(5) The patrol leader must establish control measures, alternate withdrawal routes, and coordinated fire support (both from security elements within the patrol and from fire support units) to assist him in extricating the patrol if it is endangered by enemy action.

(6) It will often be necessary for reconnaissance and security elements to move by bounds until the security element can be positioned prior to the final approach by the reconnaissance element into the objective area.

c. Typical methods of conducting area reconnaissance:

SUCCESSIVE SECTORS

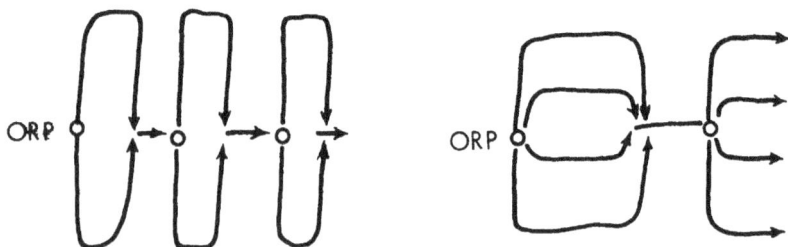

BOX METHOD   FAN METHOD

ORP   ORP   ORP

STATIONARY OBSERVATION
(may be referred to as area surveillance)

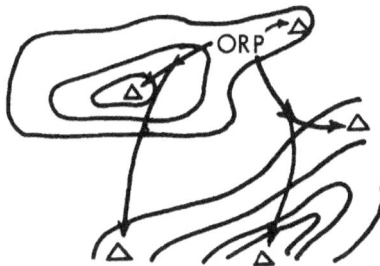

ORP

   3. The Raid Patrol. The raid patrol has the mission
to destroy or capture personnel or equipment, destroy installations, or liberate personnel.
      a. Typical organization of a raid patrol.

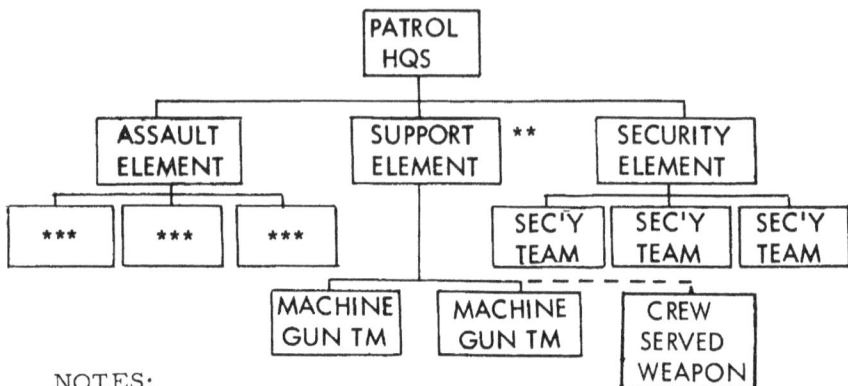

```
                    ┌──────────┐
                    │  PATROL  │
                    │   HQS    │
                    └──────────┘
        ┌────────────────┼──────── ** ──────────┐
┌──────────────┐  ┌──────────────┐      ┌──────────────┐
│   ASSAULT    │  │   SUPPORT    │      │  SECURITY    │
│   ELEMENT    │  │   ELEMENT    │      │  ELEMENT     │
└──────────────┘  └──────────────┘      └──────────────┘
 ┌──────┬──────┐                    ┌────────┬────────┬────────┐
┌────┐┌────┐┌────┐              ┌────────┐┌────────┐┌────────┐
│*** ││*** ││*** │              │ SEC'Y  ││ SEC'Y  ││ SEC'Y  │
└────┘└────┘└────┘              │ TEAM   ││ TEAM   ││ TEAM   │
                                └────────┘└────────┘└────────┘
        ┌──────────┬──────────┐
  ┌──────────┐┌──────────┐┌──────────┐
  │ MACHINE  ││ MACHINE  ││  CREW    │
  │ GUN TM   ││ GUN TM   ││ SERVED   │
  └──────────┘└──────────┘│ WEAPON   │
                          └──────────┘
```

NOTES:

*Patrol leader normally accompanies the assault element on the objective, with his RTO. Patrol hqs (-) may remain in ORP, or be employed elsewhere to assist in control and communication.

**If suitable terrain from which to provide support is not available in the objective area, the support element may be combined with the assault element, and accompany it in the assault.

***Within the assault element, special teams are organized in accordance with the mission, for example, demo team, search team, carrying team, prisoner team, etc.

     b. Planning considerations, raid patrol.

     (1) Raid operations are planned to employ maximum use of surprise. If a raid patrol fails to use sufficient stealth and patience, or fails to make thorough preparations for the attack, surprise may be lost and chances of success seriously jeopardized.

     (2) The organization of the raid patrol for actions at the objective and the plan for these actions must

provide for the efficient and rapid accomplishment of the mission.

(3) Quick, efficient accomplishment of a raid mission depends on (a) a heavy volume of surprise fire when the attack is initiated to achieve fire superiority immediately, and (b) organization and control of actions in the objective area to accomplish all actions required by the mission without delay or confusion. Some form of rehearsal is essential.

(4) Prior to the attack, a leader's recon is conducted to determine approach routes, security positions, support weapons positions, assault team positions, release points, withdrawal routes, and location of the ORP. After this has been done the original plan must be tailored to conform to the actual terrain and enemy situation.

(5) Once the attack is initiated the patrol secures the objective area only long enough to accomplish its mission and then withdraws without delay. Delay in the objective area exposes the patrol to the superior force which the enemy will usually be able to bring into play by reinforcing or counterattacking.

(6) Withdrawal must be planned in advance to allow the patrol to break contact and move quickly, undetected by the enemy, to a pre-selected location even if the withdrawal starts under enemy pressure.

(7) A simple plan, thoroughly rehearsed and vigorously executed, offers the best chance of success.

(8) The plan should be flexible, so that with the loss of surprise a smooth transition from one based on stealth to one based on firepower and shock action can be made.

4. The Ambush.
    a. General. The ambush is defined as a surprise attack upon a moving or temporarily halted enemy. The

6.07

ambush must have spontaneous, violent, coordinated action.

    b. Considerations of a successful ambush are:

        (1) Men must be good marksmen from all positions.

        (2) Well trained team that possesses a high standard of battle discipline.

        (3) Simple, effective plan in which each man knows his duty - if possible reconnoiter area beforehand. Use caution to avoid disclosing your intent.

        (4) All around security in all phases of the operation. Be especially careful while returning to friend-ly lines or base camp.

        (5) Placement of men and siting of weapons. Concealment is first priority.

        (6) A simple, clearly understood signal to open fire and cease firing.

    c. Area ambush. The area ambush position must have all approaches covered and must be laid out in width or depth. An ambush patrol may consist of small teams, each self-contained, with a leader and own security.

        (1) Typical organization - Area ambush:

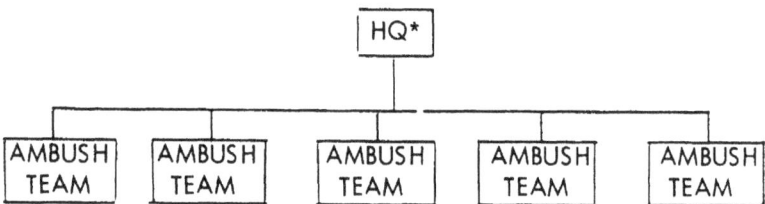

```
                        ┌──────┐
                        │ HQ*  │
                        └──┬───┘
                           │
  ┌──────┬──────┬──────────┴────┬──────┬──────┐
┌──────┐┌──────┐┌──────┐   ┌──────┐┌──────┐
│AMBUSH││AMBUSH││AMBUSH│   │AMBUSH││AMBUSH│
│ TEAM ││ TEAM ││ TEAM │   │ TEAM ││ TEAM │
└──────┘└──────┘└──────┘   └──────┘└──────┘
```

*Normally will accompany one of the ambush teams in the objective area.

(2) Typical employment - Area ambush:

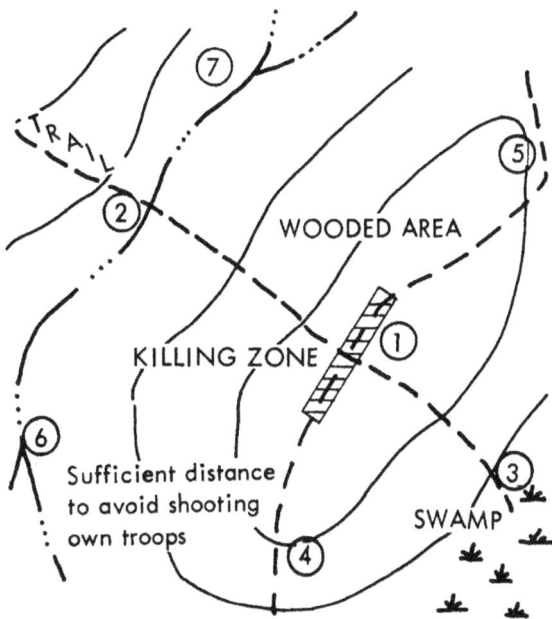

Figure 1. (See Note Below)

NOTE: Information received indicates guerrillas will meet
in edge of swamp near woodline at trail junction.
They may arrive along trail through woods or along
trail in woodline. Patrol is divided into teams in
order to cover all approaches into area. Unless a
team is discovered, all teams will allow guerrillas to pass through to team (1) which, in this example, will spring the ambush. After initial burst
of firing, the outlying teams will cut off all guerrillas attempting to escape, e.g., guerrillas may
run out of killing zone near (1) over hill along

6.09

trail into team (2), or down trail on edge of swamp toward team (4), or cross over hill to stream then into teams (6) or (7). An ambush organized similar to this example is most effective as approaches and main escape routes are covered. The ambush is organized in depth.

  d. Linear ambush. Because of terrain, there may be only one likely avenue of approach, and the ambush patrol may be together or in teams along the road or trail is ordered to give width and all-around defense. The patrol must take advantage of adequate concealment. This is termed the linear ambush and is used when the situation and terrain permits, or as part of an area ambush, along approach or escape routes. The "L" or "V", etc., types are variations of this basic linear ambush.
  (1) Typical organization - Linear Ambush.

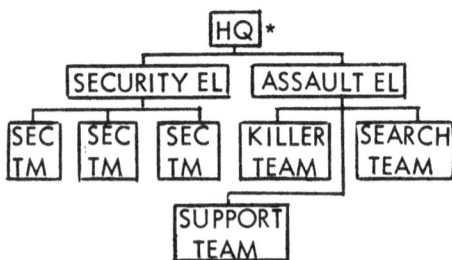

```
                        ┌────┐
                        │ HQ │ *
                        └────┘
              ┌────────────┴────────────┐
        ┌───────────┐            ┌──────────┐
        │SECURITY EL│            │ASSAULT EL│
        └───────────┘            └──────────┘
      ┌─────┬────┬────┐        ┌──────┬──────┐
    ┌────┐┌────┐┌────┐      ┌──────┐┌──────┐
    │SEC ││SEC ││SEC │      │KILLER││SEARCH│
    │TM  ││TM  ││TM  │      │TEAM  ││TEAM  │
    └────┘└────┘└────┘      └──────┘└──────┘
                  └──────────────┘
                   ┌────────┐
                   │SUPPORT │
                   │ TEAM   │
                   └────────┘
```

*Normally will accompany the assault element at the objective.

6.10

(2) Typical Employment - Linear Ambush.

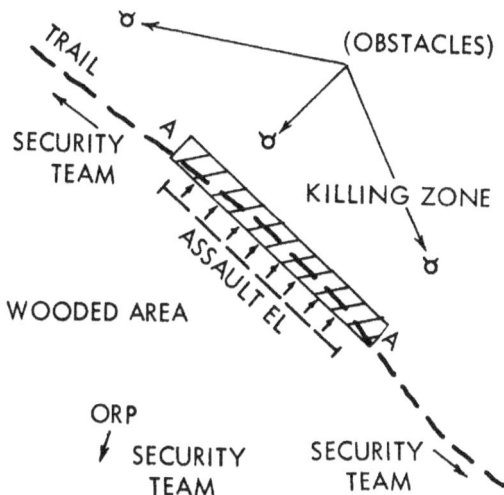

Figure 2. (See Note Below)

NOTE: An enemy patrol may approach along trail. The patrol leader decided to ambush in vicinity of (A) (killing zone). Assault element has support, "killer" and search teams. Security teams are positioned on flanks to provide early warning and to cut-off enemy escaping from the killing zone. These teams might ambush a relief force coming from either direction. A security team would occupy the ORP and if necessary, be subdivided to form a protective screen in rear of patrol. Mines footspikes, etc., are placed on far side of KZ-forming an obstacle along this escape route.

e. Vehicular ambush: Ambushing of an enemy column of vehicles can be organized similar to a linear ambush.

6. 11

(1) Typical organization - Vehicular Ambush.

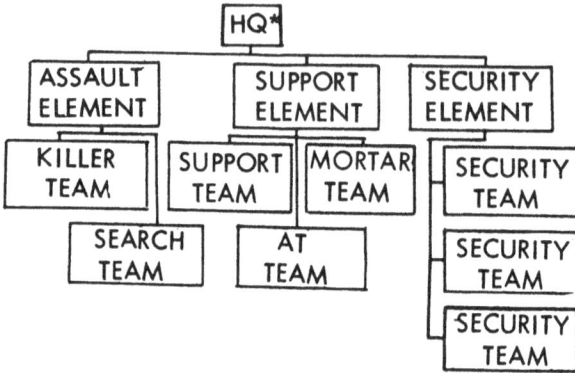

```
                    ┌─────┐
                    │ HQ* │
                    └──┬──┘
        ┌──────────────┼──────────────┐
   ┌─────────┐   ┌─────────┐   ┌─────────┐
   │ ASSAULT │   │ SUPPORT │   │SECURITY │
   │ ELEMENT │   │ ELEMENT │   │ ELEMENT │
   └────┬────┘   └────┬────┘   └────┬────┘
   ┌─────────┐ ┌─────────┐┌────────┐ ┌─────────┐
   │ KILLER  │ │ SUPPORT ││ MORTAR │ │SECURITY │
   │  TEAM   │ │  TEAM   ││  TEAM  │ │  TEAM   │
   └─────────┘ └─────────┘└────────┘ └─────────┘
     ┌─────────┐    ┌────────┐       ┌─────────┐
     │ SEARCH  │    │  AT    │       │SECURITY │
     │  TEAM   │    │ TEAM   │       │  TEAM   │
     └─────────┘    └────────┘       └─────────┘
                                     ┌─────────┐
                                     │SECURITY │
                                     │  TEAM   │
                                     └─────────┘
```

*Normally accompanies the assault element at the objec-
tive.

(2) Typical Employment - Vehicular Ambush.

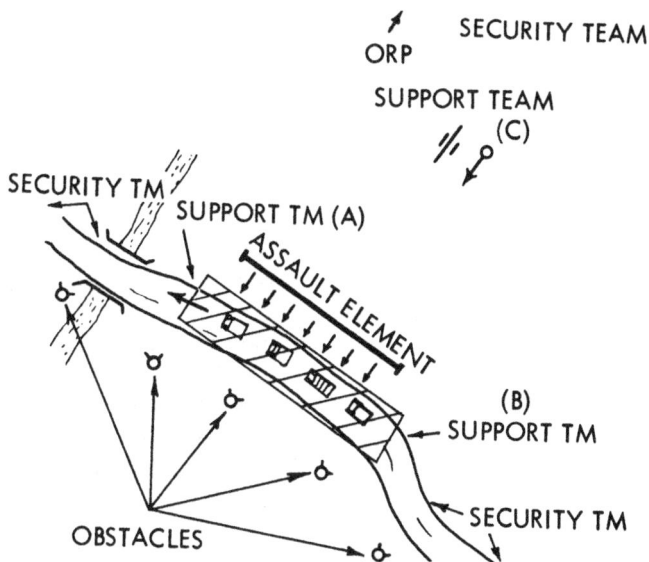

Figure 3. (See Note Below)

NOTE: Main attack force is assault element composed of
"killer" and search teams. (HQ might be with this
element.) Support element can be combined or
separated as shown, i.e., team (A) antitank weapons; (B) LMGS and grenade launchers, positioned
to have enfilade fire on the exposed portion of
vehicles; (C) indirect fire weapons. Security
teams on flanks could cover demo or obstacles and
provide early warning. One security team would

6 13

provide security in ORP or ambush reinforcement, or cut-off enemy attempting to escape from killing zone. Communications by wire, radio or other means are of great importance, especially between security teams and the HQ for early warning. Mines, foot spikes, etc., are placed on far side of KZ, forming an obstacle along that escape route.

f. Night ambush considerations are basically the same as day ambushes. Points to remember are:

(1) Use primarily area or automatic weapons.

(2) Control is vital - position men closer. Issue clear orders and signals.

(3) If at all possible, no one should move at night, so any movement can be regarded as enemy. Also wait until BMNT to reorganize, if the tactical situation permits. However, when ambushing a column of vehicles behind enemy lines, often it may be necessary to withdraw quickly and avoid detection by a superior enemy force in the area.

(4) Fix sectors of fire with stakes - understand firing instructions.

(5) Best to move into positions before EENT.

(6) Plan for illumination in case needed.

CHAPTER SEVEN

AERIAL MOVEMENT AND RESUPPLY

CONTENTS:

1. Characteristics of Army rotary-wing aircraft.
   a. Utility helicopters.

	OH-23 OH-13H	OH-6	UH-1H
Cruising speed (knots)	70	100	100
Combat-equipped troops	1	3	12
Litters	2	0	6
Parachutists	0	3	12
External sling capability (lbs)	0	0	4,000
Endurance (hrs; min)	1:45	2:25	2:15
Payload 50-NM radius (lbs)	735	1620	4900
Cargo compartment:	NA		
height (in)		20	52
width (in)		50	96
length (in)		47	92
Cargo door(s)	NA		
height (in)		40	49
width (in)		24	92

(1) The OH-13H (Sioux) and OH-23 (Raven) a two-place helicopter designed for observation, reconnaissance, medical evacuation, and general utility missions. Normally carries only one passenger in cockpit. Can transport two

litter patients in pods mounted on landing skids. May be
used to transport light, critical cargo, or to lay wire
across difficult terrain.

(2) The UH-1 (Iroquois). The standard utility
helicopter. The B and C models are used primarily for
aerial fire support, medical evacuation, or aerial command posts. The D and H models are used for light tacti
cal transport.

b. Cargo helicopters.

	CH-47B	CH-54
Cruising speed (knots)	110	100
Combat-equipped troops	33	46
Litters	24	34
Parachutists	33	46
External sling capacity (lbs)	16,000	20,760
Endurance (hrs;min)	2:40	1:45
Cargo compartment:		NA
length (in)	366	
width (in)	90	
height (in)	78	
Cargo door:		NA
width (in)	90	
height (in)	78	
Payload 50-NM radius (lbs)	15,800	22,700

7.03

(1) The CH-47B (Chinook) is a twin-engine, tandem rotor, medium transport helicopter, with fixed four-wheel landing gear. Normal crew is three, including a crew chief. A cargo winch has a 3000-pound capacity; an air rescue winch which operates through a floor hatch has a 600-pound capacity. A rear loading ramp permits straight-in loading. The sealed hull gives an emergency water landing capability.

(2) The CH-54 (Flying Crane) is a twin engine, single rotor, heavy lift helicopter. Normal crew is three, including a crew chief. A detachable pod is capable of housing a small aid station, an operations center, or carrying troops.

2. Characteristics of Army Fixed-Wing Aircraft.

	O-1	U-6A	U-1A
Cruising speed (knots)	87	105	105
ACL (lbs)	500	1000	2200
Combat Equipped troops	1	5	10
Litters	0	2	6
Parachutists	0	4	5
Takeoff distance to clear 50-ft obstacle (ft)	680	1000	1650
Landing distance to clear 50-ft obstacle (ft)	660	1050	1200
Endurance (hrs;min)	4:00	4:00	6:30
Cargo compartment:			
length (in)	NA	76	156
width (in)	NA	48	60
height (in)	NA	51	52
Cargo door:			
width (in)	NA	30	45
height (in)	NA	40	46

a. The O-1 (Birddog) is an all-metal high-wing monoplane, with conventional fixed landing gear. Two wing shackles have a 250-pound (each) capacity for carrying or parachuting cargo bundles. Two models, A and E, are essentially identical. Primary function is observation.

b. The U-6A (Beaver) is an all-metal, high-wing mono plane with conventional fixed landing gear. Four wing shackles have a 250-lb (each capacity for carrying or parachuting cargo bundles). Primary functions are personnel and cargo transport, and medical evacuation.

c. The U-1a (Otter) is a single-engine, high-wing monoplane with fixed conventional landing gear. Primary functions are transport of light cargo, air delivery, medical evacuation, and liaison.

3. Coordination with aviation representative or aircraft pilot. See Air Coordination Checklist, Chapter 2.

4. Resupply Operations:
    a. Considerations in selecting DZ for parachute delivery:
        (1) Tactically suitable--able to secure and close to route or base.
        (2) Formation and altitude--if more than one aircraft is employed, use trail. Drop altitude usually 200 feet.
        (3) Free of obstacles, and a firm surface.
        (4) Routes in and out of area for aircraft and for re ception committee.
        (5) Size of area--50 meters in length per bundle (unless bundles are dropped in salvo from door or simultaneously from wing shacles) and wide enough for some margin of error.
    b. Organization of patrol into reception committee:
        (1) Command party.
        (2) Marking party.
        (3) Security party.

7.05

     (4) Recovery party.

     (5) Transport party.

  c. Wind Drift formula and emplacement of code panels.

     (1) Drift = Constant X Altitude (Expressed in hundreds of feet) X Velocity (Ground Winds).

       (a) Drift = meters of windward drift for parachute from time of exit from aircraft to point of impact.

       (b) Constant = expressed numerical value for specific parachutes. 4.1 for T-10 parachute. 2.6 for all other parachutes.

       (c) Altitude = actual altitude of aircraft at time of airdrop. Expressed in hundreds of feet.

       (d) Wind Velocity = speed of ground wind in knots. If anemometer is not available wind should be estimated.

    EXAMPLES

       Aircraft is at altitude of 300 feet. Airdrop is rations using a G-11A parachute. Ground wind is 05 knots.

    D = KAV

       D = 2.6 (constant) X 3 (Altitude in hundreds of feet) X 5 (ground wind).

       D = 39 meters in windward direction.

     (2) Emplacement of code letter.

       (a) Determine windward drift of parachute by using wind drift formula.

       (b) Determine the desired point of impact keeping in mind those characteristics of a desirable drop zone. Move in to the wind the number of meters required (determined by drift formula) to allow for drift of parachute. From this point move the desired number of meters into the aircraft flight azimuth to compensate for forward thrust of the parachute upon exit from aircraft. The forward thrust of the parachute is determined by taking 1/2 of speed of aircraft. The answer is expressed in meters. At this point on the ground a code panel is displayed.

SEE DIAGRAM BELOW

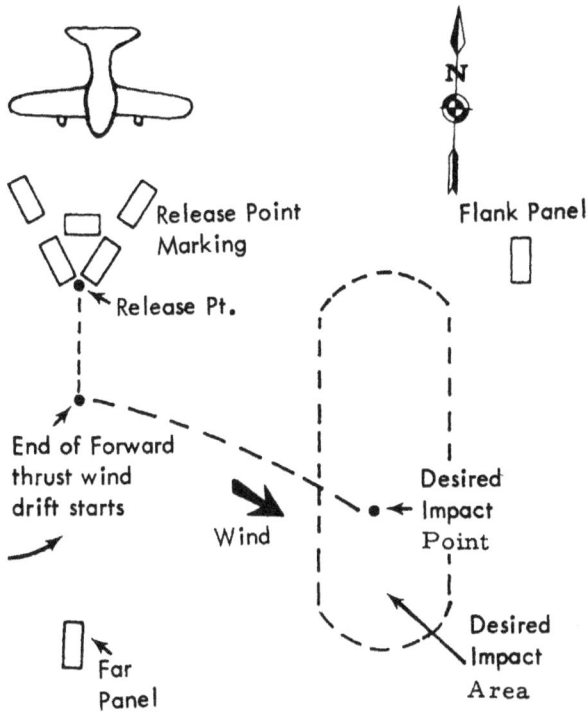

The aircraft is at 300 feet altitude, at a speed of 100 knots. Flight azimuth is 180° (north to south). The ground wind speed and direction is 05 knots from the northwest.

Prior to the drop it may be necessary to determine the dispersion pattern if more than one bundle is dropped. This is done by multiplying the number of bundles times 1/2 the speed of aircraft. The result is expressed in meters and should be a consideration in determining the length of the drop zone.

7.07

EXAMPLE: Dispersion = no. of bundles (4) X 1/2 speed of aircraft (100) k.

D = 4 X 50   D = 200M

Bundles will be spread over an area 200M long and on line with flight azimuth.

   (c) Visual Signals.
     1. Visual signals are composed of VS-17 Air Panels in hours of daylight and of flashlights, or substitutes, during hours of darkness. The configuration of the code panels, or lights, will differ in accordance with unit SOP's.
       a. US Army units normally employ any letter which composes the word HATE. This is laid out by using 5 panels or 9 lights with the exception of the code letter "T", which requires 5 lights. The lights are placed 5 meters apart with the exception of the stem of "T" in which the panels are 8 meters apart. To the left of code letter, on line with code letter, and at a distance of 200M (terrain permitting) is the flank panel. This indicates to pilot when he is directly over code letter. The long axis of panels face aircraft. The far panel is in line with code panel and flight azimuth of aircraft. This marks the end of the drop zone. This panel is placed at a maximum distance of 500M. Terrain may dictate it be moved closer to the code panel. The long axis of the panel faces the aircraft.

7.08

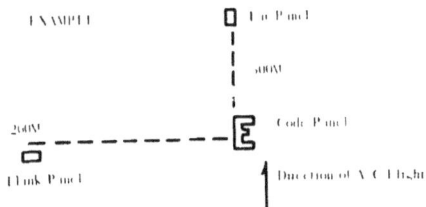

EXAMPLE

Far Panel

600M

Code Panel

200M

Flank Panel

Direction of A/C Flight

The aircraft flies on an azimuth in direct line with code letter and far panel. When directly over code letter and on line with flank panel, cargo or personnel are exited. Far and flank panels are replaced by lights during hours or darkness.

(d) The USAF employs the inverted "L". This code letter does not require a flank or far panel. It is composed of four (4) VS-17 panels during daylight or 4 flashlights or substitutes during hours of darkness.

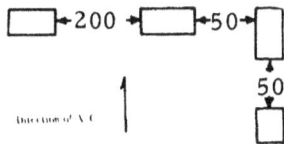

200 ← → 50 →

Direction of A/C

50

Personnel or cargo are released when on line with the flank panel offset 200M.

(e) Communications Procedures for Resupply Parachute Drops.

1. At the coordination conference a communications check point (CCP) is designated. A CCP is a

7.09

point on the ground where the aircraft pilot initiates commo with the ground personnel receiving the drop. It should be easily recognizable from air and must be within radio range It is ideally 5 miles from the DZ.

      a. The CCP is also the point on ground where ground personnel begin to relay instructions to the aircraft pilot. The pilot should alert the ground party upon reaching the CCP. If the CCP is not easily recognizable from the air it must be marked by panels or lights.

      b. The following format is used for instructions to the aircraft pilot. It is transmitted when the aircraft pilot alerts the ground party prior to reaching the CCP.

      (1) Heading _____ ° (azimuth from CCP to drop site).

      (2) Enemy situation (omit if neg).

      (3) Drop formation and drop altitude (indicated).

      (4) Maintain _____ altitude indicated until I have you in sight.

      (5) Descend to _____ (indicated drop altitude).

      (6) Steer right or left (for adjustment of aircraft flight pattern if needed).

      (7) On course.

      (8) Stand by.

      (9) Execute, Execute, Execute/No drop, no drop, no drop, (given until action is noted or aircraft has departed area.

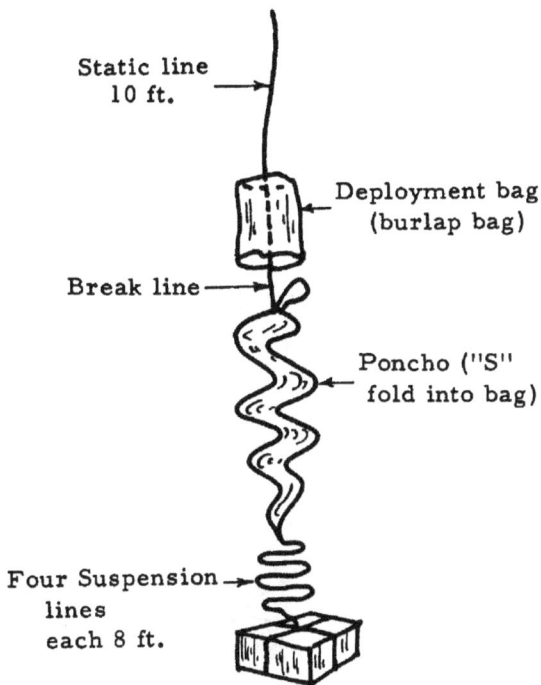

Static line
10 ft.

Deployment bag
(burlap bag)

Break line

Poncho ("S"
fold into bag)

Four Suspension
lines
each 8 ft.

Expedient Poncho Parachute - Door Bundle

7.11

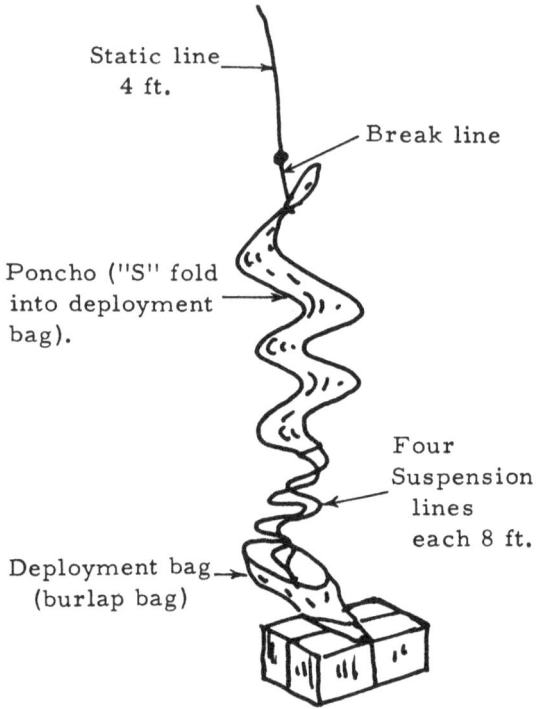

Static line
4 ft.

Break line

Poncho ("S" fold
into deployment
bag).

Four
Suspension
lines
each 8 ft.

Deployment bag
(burlap bag)

Expedient Poncho Parachute - Wing Bundle

7.12

5. Helicopter Operations.
   a. Standard helicopter section formations:

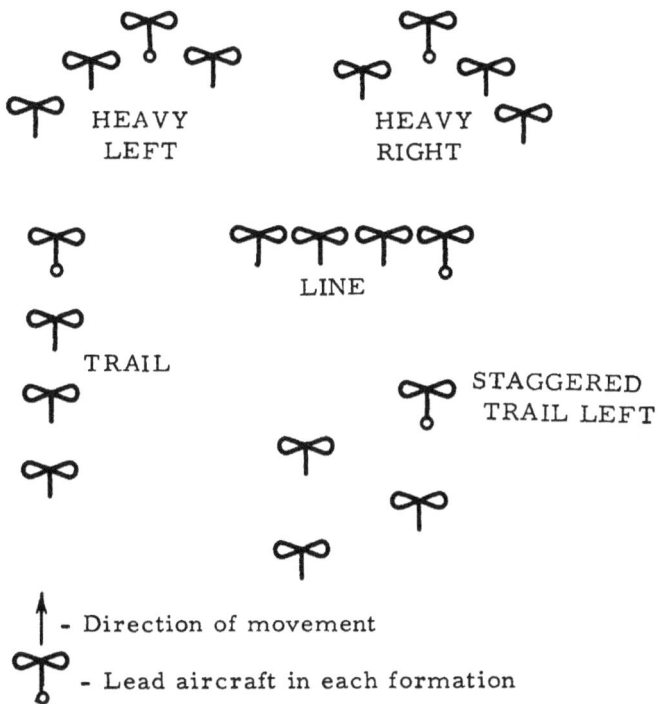

HEAVY
LEFT

HEAVY
RIGHT

LINE

TRAIL

STAGGERED
TRAIL LEFT

↑ - Direction of movement

- Lead aircraft in each formation

Required distance between aircraft--50 meters from side to side, 70 meters from front to rear.

b. Considerations in selecting LZ:

    (1) Tactical suitability.

    (2) Number and type aircraft, formation, and altitude affect the size of area required.

        (a) Circular open area 60 meters in diameter for one helicopter.

        (b) 50 meters between aircraft on line or echelon, and 70 meters if in trail (for CH-47 more distance is needed).

        (c) 10:1 ratio of take-off and landing distance to obstacle height for most Army helicopters. At high altitudes above sea level, more distance is needed.

    (3) Free of obstacles and level (maximum slope is 15 percent).

    (4) Routes in and out of area for aircraft and for patrol.

c. Use of visual signals at a helicopter LZ:

    (1) Day: The only signals required are a signalman, smoke and red panels to mark obstacles which the helicopter(s) must avoid. The signalman positions himself to guide the lead helicopter to its touchdown point as it approaches into the wind.

    (2) Night: Touchdown point of lead helicopter or single helicopter is marked by a "T", other touchdown points by a single light. Obstacles are marked by a red light. Touchdown point and "T" lights may be clear or any color but red. Helicopters land just to left of "T" stem or or single light, as applicable. See diagram below. (o = light, x = touchdown point)

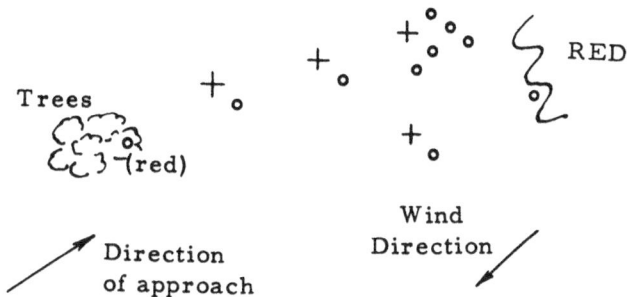

Trees

Direction
of approach

Wind
Direction

RED

d. Communications procedure--helicopter landing.
    (1) Heading (azimuth).
    (2) Enemy situation (omit if negative).
    (3) Wind _____(direction) AT_____(knots).
    (4) Land formation (formation for landing).
    (5) Land azimuth (into the wind).
    (6) Field elevation (from map).
    (7) Clear to land.
  e. Hand and arm signals for guiding helicopter landings
(all signals must be given in a clear, distinct manner):

APPROACH:

(Arms extended above
head, palms in, indi-
cates aircraft glide
path is good, continue
approach.)

WAVE OFF,
GO AROUND
   OR
STOP

(Wave arms from side
to side overhead.)

7.15

HOVER:		(Arms extended horizontally sideways, palms down.)
MOVE AHEAD:		Arms a little aside, palms facing backwards and repeatedly moved upwards and backwards from shoulder height.
MOVE BACK:		Arms by side, palms facing forward, arms swept forward and upward repeatedly to shoulder height.
MOVE RIGHT:		(Left arm extended sideways, right arm swung in front of body to indicate direction of movement-- repeated as necessary.)
MOVE LEFT:		(Right arm extended sideways, left arm swung in front of body to indicate direction of movement-- repeated as necessary.)

7.16

MOVE UPWARDS:

(Arms extended to side with palms up, motioning upwards (speed of movement indicates rate of ascent.)

MOVE DOWNWARDS:

(Arms extended to side with palms down, motioning downward (speed of movement indicates rate of descent.)

TAKE OFF:

(Make circular motion with right hand overhead, ending in throwing motion in direction of take-off.)

LAND:

(Arms extended downwards and crossed in front of body.)

CUT ENGINES:

(Draw extended fingers of one hand across neck in throat cutting motion.)

7.17

f. Helicopter loading and unloading checklist.
   (1) Preloading operations:
      (a) Personal gear tied down and checked.
      (b) Short antennas placed on radios.
      (c) Personnel tactically dispersed. However, all personnel must be able to see P. L's hand and arm signals.
      (d) Coordinate loading with crew chief.
      (e) Element and team leaders check their men's equipment to insure it is complete.
      (f) Radios on and communications checks performed (unless otherwise directed).
   (2) Loading of aircraft:
      (a) **Load helicopters on the double with interval between men.**
      (b) Load by teams, 1/2 covering, 1/2 moving. P. L. controlling by hand and arm signals, while kneeling near door.
      (c) Patrol leader last man aboard. Normally, seated behind the pilot in the UH-1D and H.
      (d) Keep doorways clear.
      (e) Bayonets will not be fixed in the aircraft.
      (f) Weapons safeties on while aboard.
      (g) Seat belts fastened. As required.
      (h) Loading more than one aircraft is done simultaneously.
   (3) Landing and unloading:
      (a) Unfasten seat belts on crew chiefs command.

(b) Unloading does not begin until directed by crew chief or pilot. Individuals remain seated until man next to them starts moving.

(c) Clear aircraft quickly and go into initial formation.

(d) Check that all equipment is off the aircraft.

(e) Release the aircraft.

6. Ground-Air Emergency Code:

1	Require doctor, serious injures	I
2	Require medical supplies	II
3	Unable to proceed	X
4	Require food and water	F
5	Require firearms and ammunition	⋁
6	Require map and compass	□
7	Require signal lamp with battery and radio	ı̇
8	Indicate direction to proceed	K
9	Am proceeding in this direction	↑
10	Will attempt takeoff	⊳
11	Aircraft seriously damaged	L⌐
12	Probably safe to land here	△

13 Require fuel and oil	L
14 All well	L L
15 No	N
16 Yes	Y
17 Not understood	⌐L
18 Require engineer	W

NOTE: A space of 10 feet between elements whenever possible.

CHAPTER EIGHT

FIRE SUPPORT

PART ONE - ARTILLERY

1. GENERAL. The proper use of fire support greatly increases a patrol's capability to accomplish its mission. In order to be effective, fire support must be planned and coordinated prior to actually undertaking a mission. Fire support should be planned not only on the objective but also on the patrol's route so it may be used should the patrol encounter unexpected trouble or require orientation.

2. CAPABILITIES.

WEAPON	RANGE (METERS)	AMMUNITION TYPES	FUZES	IMPACT AREA* DEPTH	WIDTH	RADIUS
81mm mortar	4737	HE WP ILLUM	SQ DELAY VT	15	40	
4.2in mortar	5650	HE WP ILLUM	SQ DELAY VT	20	25	
105mm howitzer	11000	HE, CML ILLUM HEAT SMOKE ANTI-PERS	QUICK DELAY VT, TIME CONCRETE PIERCING	20	30	175
155mm howitzer	14600	HE, CML ILLUM SMOKE	QUICK DELAY VT, TIME CONCRETE PIERCING	30	50	360
8-in. howitzer	16800	HE NUCLEAR	QUICK DELAY VT, TIME CONCRETE PIERCING	30	80	470
175mm gun	32800	HE	QUICK DELAY VT	35	95	518

*Depth and width describe area of effective coverage. Radius indicates area within which large fragments may be effective.

3. CATEGORIES OF FIRE. There are two types of targets.
    a. Planned targets.
        (1) Scheduled targets - These targets are pre-planned with regard to time and location. They may require no communication between supported unit and artillery unit.
        (2) On-call targets - These targets are planned as to location and are requested by the supported units as required.
    b. Targets of opportunity. These targets are requested as they appear. They are not preplanned, but may be designated using preplanned targets as a reference point.

4. GRAPHIC SYMBOLS.
    a. A single target is marked by a "tick mark." The center of the tick mark gives the location of the target. The target is identified by a number or a name.

EXAMPLE: ⊢ Tuesday

    b. Targets of linear configuration may be designated by a linear symbol.

EXAMPLE: | Wednesday |

    c. Area targets may be designated using an area plot.

EXAMPLE: (Friday)

    d. Two or more targets which may be fired simultaneously may be included in a group of targets. The individual targets are designated separately so they can be fired individually. The group is given a separate designation.

EXAMPLE: (Saturday ⊢   Sunday ⊢)
                    Weekend
GROUPS OF TARGETS
8.02

5. FIRE PLANNING.
   a. Fire support is planned to:
   DESTROY enemy troops and equipment.
   DECEIVE the enemy as to patrol's location and
intentions.
   DENY the enemy freedom of movement and observation.
   DEFEND the patrol while in a patrol or combat
base or in the event of an unplanned encounter.
   DIRECT the patrol during their movement by
firing marking rounds.
   DELAY enemy reinforcement and pursuit.
   b. Route fires. Targets are planned along all
routes which the patrol anticipates using. These targets
should be planned on known or suspected positions which
might engage the patrol. They are also planned on danger
areas. They may also be planned as navigational aids and
to cover the patrols movement.
   c. Objective fires. Targets should be planned on
and beyond the objective. These targets will assist the
patrol in assaulting and/or destroying the objective. Targets are also planned on likely avenues of approach to the
objective to prevent reinforcement or escape of the enemy
forces. They may also be used to cover the patrol's withdrawal. These targets may be fired as a group of targets
or a series of targets.
   d. Counterguerrilla employment. Fires against
guerrilla forces will normally fall into the target of opportunity category. Planned targets should still be established
on prominent terrain features and likely points of contact
in the area of counterguerrilla operation to facilitate the
shifting of accurate planned fires on these targets of opportunity.
   e. When it is desired to fire two or more targets
and/or groups of targets in some prearranged order to support a maneuver, this may be done with a series of targets.
This series is also given a separate designation.

EXAMPLE:

SERIES
OF
TARGETS

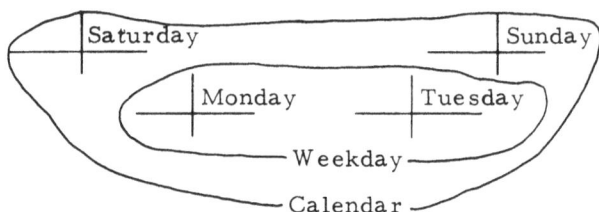

Saturday Sunday

Monday Tuesday

Weekday

Calendar

6. OVERLAY TECHNIQUES.

a. Overlays are used to show the supporting artillery the targets which have been planned to support a patrol's operation.

b. The following information is essential in making an overlay:

(1) Name, official capacity and unit of person making overlay.

(2) Map sheet which overlay pertains to.

(3) Time and date overlay was prepared.

(4) Purpose of the overlay.

(5) Tick marks to position overlay.

(6) Route.

(7) Target designations.

(8) Target list. (see example overlay)

c. The following additional information may be included on the overlay. In any case, it must be coordinated.

(1) Effective period of overlay.

(2) Call signs and frequency for communications with the patrol.

(3) Phase lines and check points to be used by the patrol.

(4) Code words to be used by the patrol.

(5) Emergency signals for fire.

d. Sample fire support overlay.

Patrol_____ Co (Ranger)75th Inf
Patrol Leader _____
Date _____
Map: Buena Vista, 1:50,000

Time of Departure: 2100
Time of Return: NLT 0400
Code Word-Alt Freq: Blackball
Code Word-Alt Rt: Romeo
Emer Sig-Tues: Red Star and Green Star
ORP location: 16889427
PL Red: Clear FEBA, before sec. halt
PL White: Complete Leader's Recon
PL BLUE: Depart ORP to FEBA
PL Green: Halt before reentry
Freq & Call Sign: 53.2/Birddog 12
Alt Freq: 51.1
—— Route to Objective
--- Return Route

TARGET LIST

	DESCRIPTION	LOCATION	REMARKS	CODE NAMES
1.	Suspect enemy emplace- ment	15469177	ILL on Call	Sunday
2.	Antitank Gun	15209345	Smoke on Call	Monday
3.	Enemy Base Camp	17239455	WP and HE	Tuesday
4.	Dam	15619261		Wednesday
5.	Dam	16729344		Thursday
6.	Road-Stream Junction	16189394		Friday
7.	Road Junction	15089253		Saturday

8. 05

7. ADJUSTMENT OF ARTILLERY FIRE.

a. In many cases, an artillery FO will not be present and the patrol leader will have to call for and adjust artillery fire.

b. Preparation of fire request. The location of the target may be given in any manner understood by both the observer and the fire direction center. Normally one of the following methods is used:

(1) Grid coordinates - Determine the grid coordinates of the target and send in the clear.

(2) Shift - Fire is shifted from a registration point, reference point, preplanned target, or other point known to both observer and FDC. The shift is announced as so many meters RIGHT or LEFT and so many beyond (ADD) or short (DROP) of the reference point. Example: FROM REGISTRATION POINT, RIGHT 600, DROP 400. The observer-target azimuth is an essential element of the shift request.

(3) Polar coordinates - If the observer's location is known to FDC, the initial location of the target may be reported by giving the direction and distance from the observer. Example: DIRECTION 3200 DISTANCE 600.

(4) If target location cannot be given, a marking round may be used as the point from which to shift fire. Example: MARK CENTER OF SECTOR or MARK REGISTRATION POINT.

c. Fire requests.

(1) Example of fire request using grid coordinates:

"RED-LEG 15, THIS IS RED-LEG 31".....	Call signs of the FDC and observer.
"FIRE MISSION"	Warning to alert the artillery unit.
"GRID 135246"...............	Determine as accurately as possible.
"DIRECTION 350"...............	Grid azimuth to the target.
"2 MACHINE GUNS FIRING".........	Description of the target.
"VT"	Air bursts will produce maximum casualties. Adjustment is made with fuze quick; fuze VT will be fired in fire for effect.
"ADJUST FIRE"................	Exact target location is doubtful, fire will be adjusted to the target location.

(2) Example of fire request using polar coordinates:

"RED-LEG 3, THIS IS RED-LEG 27"	Call signs of the FDC and observer.
"FIRE MISSION"	Warning order.
"DIRECTION 250"...............	Grid azimuth to the target.
"DISTANCE 3500"...............	Distance from the observer to the target.
"INFANTRY PLATOON IN WOODS"	This target is best attacked by air bursts. Fuze VT will burst above the tree canopy and be ineffective. Fuze quick will burst on contact with trees and produce the desired air bursts. Since fuze quick is always fired when no fuze is specified, this element is omitted.
"AT MY COMMAND, ADJUST FIRE"	The observer will command "FIRE" for each adjustment. To remove this restruction command, "CANCEL AT MY COMMAND."

(3) Example of fire request when shifting from a known point:

"RED-LEG 15, THIS IS DO-BOY 6"	Call signs of the FDC and the infantry company commander.
"FIRE MISSION"	Warning order.
"FROM TARGET AK4306"	Point from which the shift will be made. The FDC must know the location of this target.
"DIRECTION 5470"..............	Grid azimuth to the target.
"LEFT 120"	The target is located 120 meters to the left of the target and at the same range. Lateral shift or range correction can be omitted when not needed.
"INFANTRY PLATOON IN THE OPEN"	Target description indicates size and type.
"VT"	Air bursts are most effective against personnel without overhead cover. No height of burst adjustment is necessary with fuze VT.
"FIRE FOR EFFECT"	Surprise fire is desired, location is accurately known.

(4) Example of subsequent fire request (correction after first round has landed:

THIS IS RED DOG 6

RIGHT 100, ADD 200

(5) Example of subsequent fire request (final correction which will bring rounds within 50 meters of the target):

THIS IS RED DOG 6

LEFT 50 DROP 50

FIRE FOR EFFECT

(6) When fire for effect is completed, observer sends either:

END OF MISSION, TROOPS DISPERSED, 4 CASUALTIES (report of results).

or: REPEAT (If additional fires needed to accomplish mission), or: DROP 200. REPEAT, (if additional fires on new location needed).

d. In making fire requests, remember the following:

(1) Corrections are facilitated by using the "Worm" formula, W = RM. Binoculars are used to measure the mil angle.

(2) Range corrections are made by bracketing or the creeping method. Each succeeding range correction is one-half the previous one. The end result is that the target is inside a 100-meter "bracket." The observer then gives FIRE FOR EFFECT, with a 50-meter range correction. The creeping method is used when friendly troops are close enough to the target to be endangered by use of the bracketing method. Subsequent range corrections are commands to DROP one-half the estimated coverage. 50 meters is the smallest range correction used.

(3) The range correction is the last element of an adjustment command.

8. Further detail is contained in FM 6-135 "Adjustment of Artillery Fire by the Combat Soldier." A through knowledge of the contents of this manual should be gained by every Ranger and every combat arms leader.

PART TWO - AIR FIRE SUPPORT

1. GENERAL: While conducting Ranger-type operations, the patrol may find itself far behind enemy lines and beyond the support of mortar or artillery fire. In this situation, it may be necessary to plan for and utilize air support.

2. TYPES OF AIR REQUESTS:
a. Preplanned request: A preplanned request is made when a need for air support can be predicted at some future time.
b. Immediate request: An immediate request by its very nature cannot be preplanned. For example, a patrol leader may make an immediate request when he encounters a target suitable for close air support which he previously had not considered.

3. COORDINATION:
a. A preplanned or immediate request for close air support contains enough information to determine the suitability of the request. Also, it provides the Air Force with the basis for determining the armament appropriate for the mission. As a minimum, it includes:
(1) Target location.
(2) Target description (in detail).
(3) Results desired.
(4) Time over target (time target is to be hit and/or latest time acceptable).
(5) Means of control (i.e., visual or electronic).

4. METHODS OF TARGET IDENTIFICATION:
a. Colored smoke, dropped by preceding aircraft, fired by artillery, mortar or recoilless rifles, can be used as a reference point to mark the target.
b. Colored panels may be used to identify friendly troops, and give the pilot the general direction of attack. Color code of the day is required to prevent compromising location and insure identification.
c. Map coordinates of the target can be given to the strike pilot. Coordination must be made to insure both the patrol leader and pilot have the same map and coordinate system.
d. Simulated attack runs may be made if the pilot is not sure of the target. He attacks the position he thinks

8.09

is the target but does not drop the load. From this you can adjust by verbal command to move him on target.

　　e.　Land marks and terrain features can be used as a reference point from which the target may be pointed out to the pilot. Give direction and distance to target from reference point.

　　f.　The clock method requires prestrike coordination between controller and pilot. Use aircraft inbound heading as the 12 o'clock position; then indicate the distance from the aircraft to the target and the hour position for the direction.

　　g.　The "flaming arrow" technique may be used to identify friendly troops, and give pilots the direction of the enemy during hours of darkness when friendly troops are in a static position. #10 cans or similar containers are placed in an arrow configuration in a make-shift frame which can be rotated in any direction. The containers are filled with sand or dirt which is saturated with gasoline. In the event of enemy contact, the containers can be lighted and the frame rotated so that the "flaming arrow" points to the enemy force. Combined with ground-to-air communications which permit giving distances and making corrections, this method will accurately locate enemy targets for close air support pilots.

　　5.　PROCEDURE:

　　a.　Preplanned requests are normally coordinated with the S3 Air at the headquarters to which the patrol is attached. Incorporate into the fire support annex of the patrol order.

　　b.　Immediate requests are made by calling the request in to headquarters over the patrol's radios.

　　c.　An alternate means is to relay the request through an aircraft with which the patrol's radio will net (Army aircraft) and which, in turn, can net with the attack aircraft.

6. TARGET SELECTION:
a. The general principle is to select those targets for air strikes which are beyond a reasonable capability of available ground force weapons.

b. In determining whether ground targets are suitable for air attack, certain factors must be considered.
(1) Capabilities of weapons organic to the aircraft.
(2) Armament capabilities (i.e., napalm, rockets, bombs, etc.).
(3) Time is an important factor with respect to urgency of the desired results.
(4) Target identification.

7. COMMUNICATION PROCEDURES:
a. Establish communications with flight leader or FAC.

b. Request ordnance report (to determine type of ordnance aboard aircraft).

c. Give air briefing to flight or FAC (short transmissions for each paragraph below).
(1) Target description and location (give target marking method, if used) (mark your location only if necessary to establish a reference point from which target location can be identified for pilot).
(2) Terrain (covering type and hazards to flight such as hills, box canyons).
(3) Enemy ground-to-air fire (small amrs, flak).
(4) Alternate frequencies to use in event of lost radio contact.
(5) Target and friendly troop separation distance.

d. Recommended priority of expenditure of ammunition (heaviest load first unless situation dictates otherwise).

e. Recommend direction of pull-out (best general approach is from friendly side toward target--never from target into friendly troops).

f. Advise pilots of fire adjustment, as required, for succeeding passes.

g. Exchange estimates of strike results with flight leader.

h. Pass strike results to Army unit commander.

CHAPTER NINE

BOOBY TRAPS

1. ISSUE DEVICES.

    a. Pressure firing device M1A1 activated by 20 pounds pressure, utilizes standard base.

    b. Pull firing device M1 activated by pull of 3 to 5 pounds thru about 1/32". Utilizes standard base.

    c. Pressure release firing device M5. Requires 5 lb load. Activated when load is removed. Utilizes standard base.

    d. Pull release firing device M3.

        (1) Pull operation activated by pull of 6 to 10 pounds.

        (2) Release operation activated by release of taut trip wire. Utilizes standard base.

2. EXPEDIENT DEVICES.

a. Open loop. This is the only break in a complete circuit connecting an electric cap and a power source. A variety of action could pull the bare wires together.

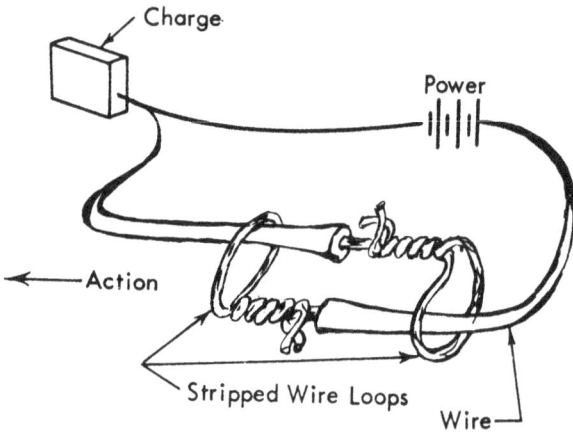

Charge

Power

Action

Stripped Wire Loops

Wire

b. Clothespin. The wooden wedge between the contacts on the jaws is the only break in a circuit connecting a cap and a power source. Removal of the wedge completes the circuit.

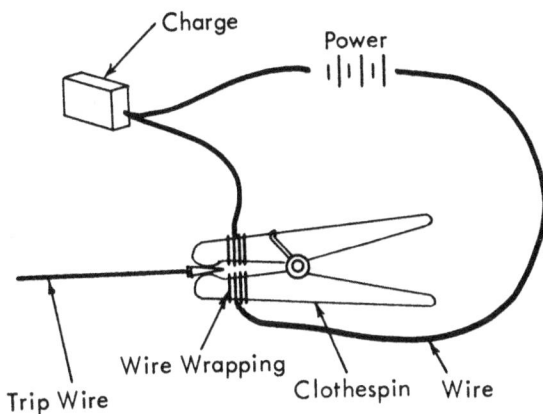

9.03

c. Pressure device can be made by punching holes in two pieces of metal. An electric lead is fastened to each piece. They are placed with the jagged edges facing each other with a piece of paper between, forming the only break in a circuit connecting an electric cap and a power source. Pressure on the top piece will puncture the paper and complete the circuit.

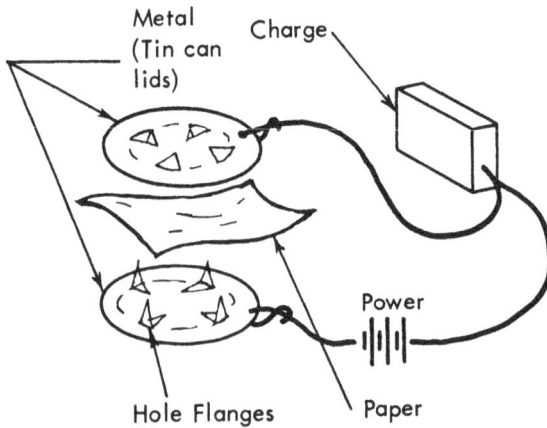

Metal (Tin can lids)

Charge

Hole Flanges

Paper

Power

d. A pressure release device can be made by removing the pin from a hand grenade and allowing the booby
trap bait to restrain the arming lever. Removal of the bait
will free the arming lever.

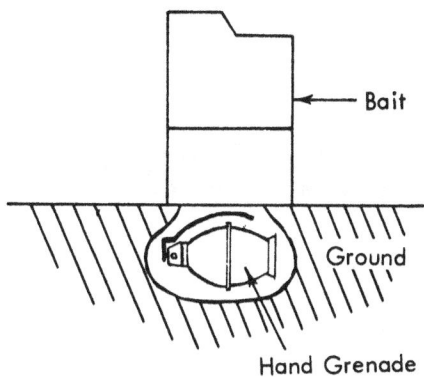

Bait

Ground

Hand Grenade

9.05

e. A release of tension device can be made by stretching a coil spring and attaching a nail with an electric lead to each end. Nails must be insulated from the spring. Release of the spring will bring the nails together completing a circuit between the power source and an electric cap.

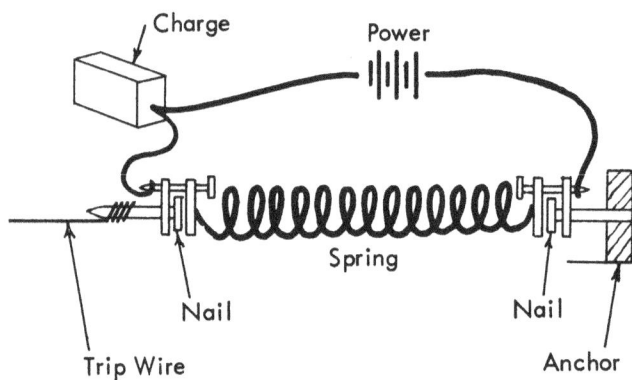

9.06

CHAPTER TEN

DEMOLITIONS

1. This chapter is to be used in conjunction with demolition card (GTA 5-10-9).

2. ADVANCED DEMOLITIONS.
    a. Pole Charge.
        (1) Principal use - to extend reach.
        (2) Dual prime.
        (3) Breaks in detonation cord are for carrying safety. Tie breaks with square knots when ready to fire.

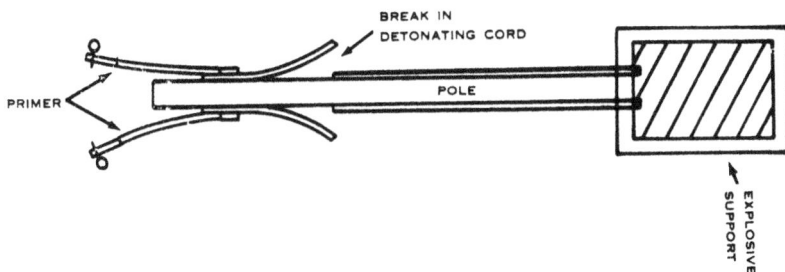

b. Improvised Shaped Charge.
        (1) Principal use - to penetrate.
        (2) Dimensions.
            (a) Stand-off distance - 1 1/2 times diameter of cone.
            (b) Height (explosive depth) - 2 times height of cone.
            (c) Angle of cone - 30 to 60 degrees.
            (d) Penetration - approximately 1 inch of steel per inch of cone diameter.
        (3) Detonation - exact rear center, dual prime.

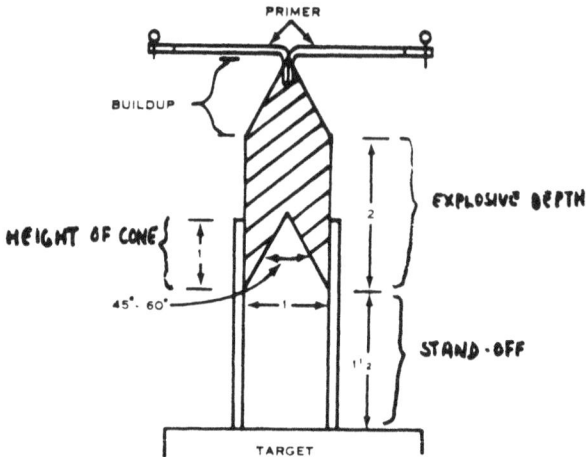

c. Ribbon Charge.
  (1) Principal use - to cut steel.
  (2) Dimensions:
    (a) Length - length of cut desired.
    (b) Width - 2 times the thickness of the
target.
    (c) Thickness - equal to the thickness of
the target; never less than 1/2 inch.
  (3) Preparation: Build up the end to be primed
if the charge is relatively thin. Build up corners if the
charge is designed to cut a target such as an I-beam.
Tamping is unnecessary. Effective only against targets
up to two inches thick.
  (4) Detonation: From either end, not both,
dual prime.

10. 02

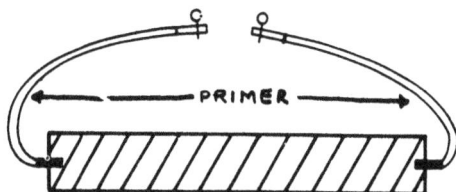

d. Linear Shaped Charge.
    (1) Principal use - to cut steel.
    (2) Dimensions:
        (a) Length - length of cut desired.
        (b) Width - same as thickness of target.
        (c) Height - one-half the thickness of the
target; at least 1/2 inch.
        (3) Preparation: Form a groove with sides
from 45 to 60 degrees down the length of the charge to
achieve the shaped-charge effect. Position the groove on
the desired line of cut.
        (4) Detonation: From either end, not both;
insure adequate explosive around caps, dual prime.

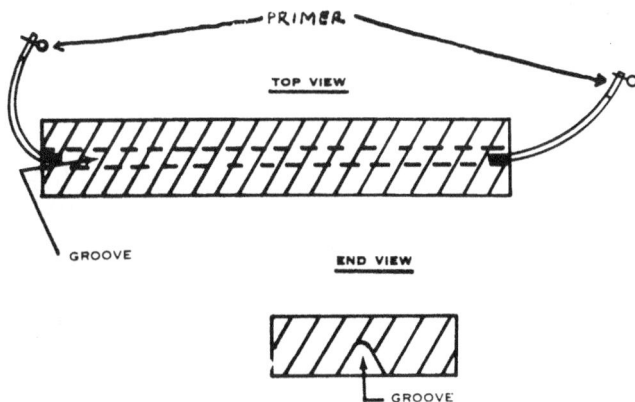

10.03

e. Diamond Charge.

(1) Principal use - to cut high carbon steel
shafts.

(2) Dimensions:

(a) Long axis - equal to circumference of
target.

(b) Short axis - 1/2 of long axis.

(c) Thickness - 2/3 inch.

(3) Preparation: Considerable time and care
required. Transferring the charge dimensions to a tem-
plate of carboard or cloth permits easier construction
(working directly on the target is extremely difficult). The
completed wrapped charge is then transferred to the target and taped or tied in place, insuring maximum close
contact.

(4) Detonation: Both points of the short axis
must be primed for simultaneous detonation. This can be
accomplished electrically or by use of equal lengths of
detonating cord, with caps crimped on the ends inserted
into the charge.

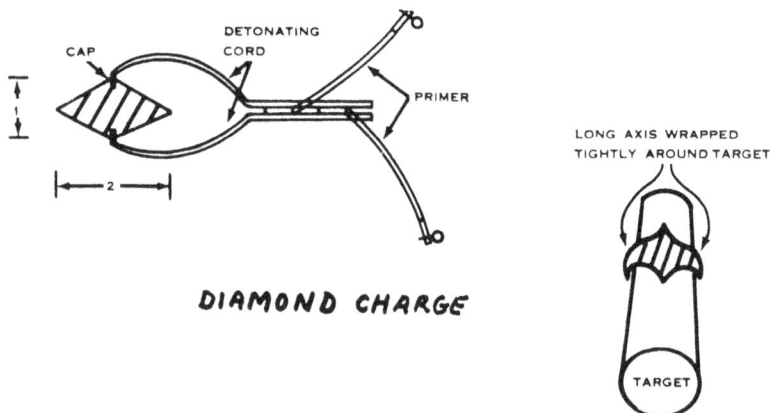

DIAMOND CHARGE

LONG AXIS WRAPPED
TIGHTLY AROUND TARGET

f. Saddle Charge.
   (1) Principal use - to cut solid steel shafts up to 8 inches in diameter.
   (2) Dimensions: as shown in diagram.
   (3) Preparation: Same considerations apply as for diamond charge.
   (4) Detonation: From apex of triangle, dual prime.

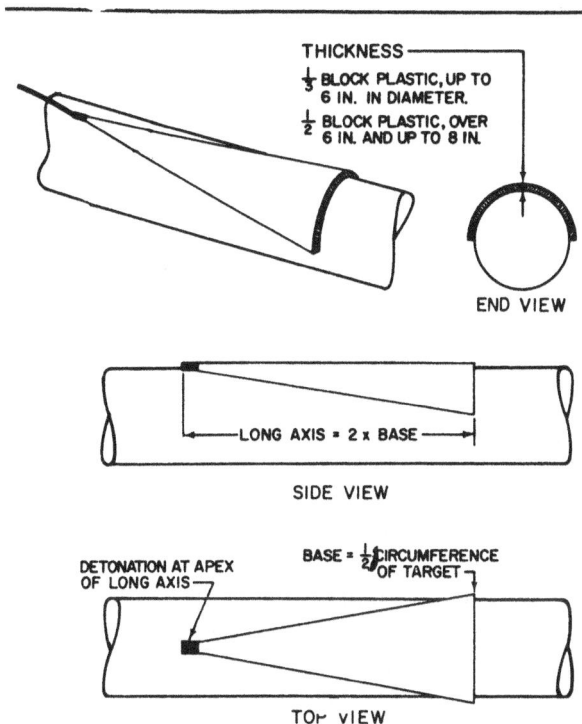

THICKNESS
$\frac{1}{3}$ BLOCK PLASTIC, UP TO 6 IN. IN DIAMETER.
$\frac{1}{2}$ BLOCK PLASTIC, OVER 6 IN. AND UP TO 8 IN.

END VIEW

LONG AXIS = 2 x BASE

SIDE VIEW

DETONATION AT APEX OF LONG AXIS

BASE = $\frac{1}{2}$ CIRCUMFERENCE OF TARGET

TOP VIEW

Saddle Charge

10.05

g. Counterforce ("Ear-Muff") Charge.
        (1) Principal use - to shatter concrete targets 4 feet or less in thickness.
        (2) Dimensions: 1 1/2 pounds of explosive (C4) per foot of concrete. The total explosive needed is divided into two exactly equal charges.
        (3) Placement: Charges exactly opposite each other.
        (4) Detonation: Prime the two charges to detonate simultaneously. Prime in the exact rear center of each charge. Dual prime.

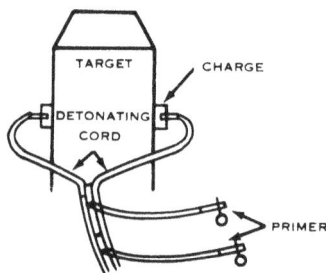

COUNTER-FORCE CHARGE

h. Sausage Charge.
        (1) Principal use - to cut timber.
        (2) Dimensions:
            (a) Length - Circumference of tree; insure ends meet.
            (b) Amount of explosive - one pound per foot of length.
        (3) Placement - place on tree at desired cut.
        (4) Detonation - at any point in charge; dual prime.

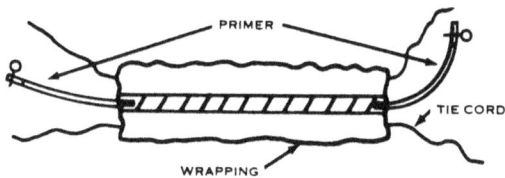

SAUSAGE CHARGE

i. Improvised Bangalore.
    (1) Principal uses - breaching wire obstacles;
producing casualties.
    (2) Dimensions:
        (a) Diameter of pipe - not larger than
two inches.
        (b) Amount of explosive - two pounds per
foot of pipe.
    (3) Preparation: Pack explosive into pipe.
Close one end with threaded cap, wooden plug or damp
earth.
    (4) Detonation: Prime from open end; dual
prime.

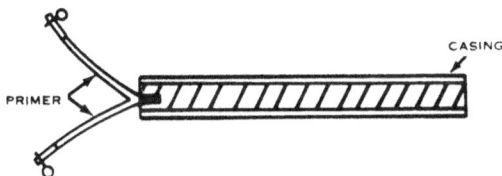

IMPROVISED BANGALORE

10.07

3. PLACEMENT.

    a. Railroads - To derail a train, at least a 20 foot section of track must be removed. Only one rail must be cut. This is best done on the outside rail of a curve. In the case of multiple tracks paralleling each other, derailment should be made in such a manner as to obstruct all tracks. If train is to be destroyed along with track, charge should be detonated in front of, not under the locomotive. The break in the track should be shunted with wire to delay detection. There are two methods of positioning charges.

    (1) Covert - 3-5-2. Three charges; one charge placed under every fifth tie with 2 lbs per charge. Difficult to install, difficult to detect.

    (2) Overt - 10-2-1. Ten charges placed against inside web of rail over every second tie; one lb per charge. Quickly installed; easily detected.

    b. Bridges.

    (1) Abutments and piers are critical in repairing bridges; destroy whenever possible.

    (2) Tension members are more difficult to replace than compression members.

    (3) Use the weight of the bridge to assist destruction.

    (4) A delay element between charges on each side of the bridge will cause a twist and hamper salvage.

    (5) When only one cut is required to cut a long member, consider using a series of smaller charges to deform member and thereby hamper reconstruction.

CHAPTER ELEVEN

FIRST AID

1. LIFESAVING STEPS (apply to all injuries.)

   a. Stop bleeding.
   b. Clear and maintain airway.
   c. Protect the wound.
   d. Prevent or treat shock.

2. TREATMENT CHART.

Problem	Symptoms	Treatment
Bleeding		Direct pressure on wound with sterile dressing. Elevate wound above heart. Use tourniquet as last resort.
Blocked Airway		Turn head to side. Extend neck. Clear all refuse from mouth.
Wounds (All)		Expose wound, control bleeding, apply sterile dressing, treat for shock. Look for wound of exit. Do not clean the wound.
Jaw Wounds		Clear and maintain airway, stop bleeding with direct pressure, do not bandage mouth shut, support jaw, position

11. 01

Problem	Symptoms	Treatment
		head to allow drainage from mouth.
Head Wounds		Elevate head. Clean the airway and protect the wound. Position head to allow drainage from mouth. DO NOT GIVE MORPHINE.
Belly Wounds		Do not touch or replace organs. Use loose, dry, sterile dressing. Give no food or liquids.
Chest Wounds		Make wound airtight immediately with plastic or foil. Cover with dry, sterile dressing. Do not give morphine.
Fractures		"Splint him where he lies." Immobilize joint above and below the break. Four ties for arm and five ties for leg minimum.
Burns	1st degree- skin is red. 2d degree- skin is blistered. 3rd degree- skin is charred and	Remove clothing. Cover burn with dry, sterile dressing or cleanest material available. Do NOT apply grease or ointment. Avoid infection. Give cool salt/

11.02

Problem	Symptoms	Treatment
	tissue de-stroyed.	soda water slowly. Treat or prevent shock.
Shock	Pale, clammy, wet skin, ner-vousness and thirst. May pass out.	Lay patient on back, elevate feet, loosen clothing, keep warm and comfortable. Feed hot liquids if conscious. Turn head to side if unconscious.
Heat exhaustion	Pale, clammy, wet skin, diz-ziness, cramps and faintness.	Move patient to shade, loosen clothing, give salt water slowly. Seek medical air.
Heat Stroke (Sun Stroke)	Dry, bright pink skin, high temperature, hot to touch, dizziness or delirium.	Lower body temperature IMMEDIATELY by immersion in stream or sprinkling water and fanning. (Use ice if available.) Seek medi-cal aid. If conscious, give cool, salt water. Evacuate as URGENT. Cool while evacuating.
Eye Injury		Cover both eyes with a dry sterile dressing.
Immersion Foot and Trench Foot	Tenderness, tissue softens, reddens and will eventually bleach.	Keep feet warm and dry. Avoid walking. Seek medical aid.

11. 03

Problem	Symptoms	Treatment
Frostbite	Grey or white skin. Frequently, no pain.	Remove clothing from effected part. Thaw in warm water. Keep casualty warm. Wrap loosely in dry, sterile dressing. Seek medical aid. Treat as litter casualty. Do not massage the area or break blisters.
Snakebite		Keep patient quiet and still. Place constricting band between bite and heart. DO NOT cut. Seek medical aid. Treat all bites as poisonous. Kill snake and evacuate with patient.
Scorpion or spider bites		Remain calm. Apply ice or immerse in cold water. Seek medical aid.
Bee or wasp sting		Treatment not usually required. Treat for shock if abnormal reaction occurs.

3. <u>Injury/Disease Prevention</u>

Problem	Prevention
Heat Injury	Gradually increase work load and exposure to heat. Eat a balanced diet. Use salt tablets only when diet is restricted. Replace water as it is lost from the body.
Cold Injury	Wear loose layers of clean, dry clothing. Avoid overheating. Exercise frequently, especially feet and toes. Change socks and massage feet frequently, each day. Use buddy system to detect and prevent cold injuries.
Foot Care	Inspect boots and socks for fit and serviceability. Keep feet clean and dry. Use foot powder. Change socks frequently. Elevate feet when possible.
Diseases	Keep body, mouth, teeth and clothing clean. Bury body wastes. Rest when possible. Keep immunizations current.

R eckless handling may kill.

A ssess extent of injuries.

N otify medics ASAP.

G ive psychological first aid.

E xtra precautions prevent disease and injury.

R emain calm.

S tay healthy to train and fight.

11. 05

CHAPTER TWELVE

FORMATIONS, DISMOUNTED

1   The file, modified column, and line are the most commonly used dismounted formations in Ranger operations.

2.   Each of these formations has certain inherent characteristics of control, security, flexibility, and speed.
       a.   Modified column:

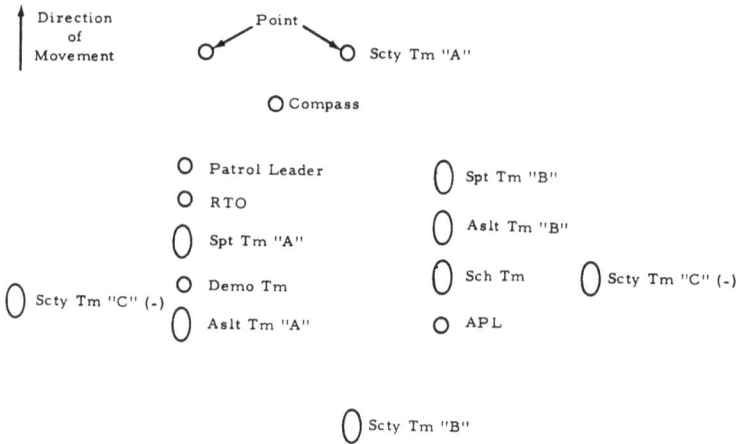

(1) Provides excellent all-around security.
(2) Good control.
(3) Flexible - can be easily changed to meet changing situations - spread for more dispersion or closed in for more control; elements easily maneuvered in meeting the enemy.
(4) Good speed.

Direction
of
Movement

Point

O ← → O

O Compass

O Patrol Leader

O RTO

O Spt Tm "A"

O Aslt Tm "A"

O Scty Tm "C" (-)   O Demo Tm   O Scty Tm "B"
                        Sch Tm

O Aslt Tm "B"

O Spt Tm "B"

O APL

O Scty Tm "C" (-)

12. 02

(1) Used when conditions of terrain or visibility are so restrictive that a column formation cannot be controlled.

(2) Control is excellent.

(3) Speed is excellent.

(4) Security and flexibility are poor.

c. Line:

(1) Basic assault formation. Also used for searching or clearing an enemy area or for crossing a short exposed area rapidly.

(2) Maximum firepower in one direction only.

(3) Control is extremely difficult.

(4) Slow moving, security to flanks and rear is very poor.

3. ORDER OF MOVEMENT.

a. Consider the following guidelines when planning your patrols order of movement:

(1) Unit integrity.

(2) All-round firepower and security.

(3) Enemy situation.

(4) Order of anticipated need.

b. The general order of movement used will be the point, compass, patrol leader, RTO, elements and teams, and assistant patrol leader near the rear for control. The point's mission is to provide frontal security. It is neither a navigational aid nor a trail-blazer.

(1) The size of the point will vary with the size of the patrol. It may be from one man to an element or squad.

(2) The point should be positioned far enough to the front to provide early warning of danger areas, and to allow the main body sufficient room to maneuver if the point encounters the enemy. This may range from a few to several hundred meters.

(3) The point moves right and left ahead of the patrol screening the area over which the patrol will pass.

The point should be made responsible for its own general navigation, and must have a thorough knowledge of the route.

CHAPTER THIRTEEN

COMBAT INTELLIGENCE

1. COMBAT INTELLIGENCE: That knowledge of the enemy, the weather, and the terrain which is used to plan and conduct tactical operations within a given area.

2. ESSENTIAL ELEMENTS OF INFORMATION (EEI). Critical items of information needed by a commander at a particular time to assist him in making a logical decision. (Combat Intelligence must include the EEI required by the commander). Generally the best information is that which is generated by the unit on the ground during operations.

3. SOURCES OF INFORMATION:
   a. Enemy activity.
   b. Prisoners of War.
   c. Local civilians.
   d. Recovered military personnel.
   e. Captured enemy documents.
   f. Captured enemy material.
   g. Refugees.

4. REPORTING INFORMATION:
   a. Report all informations as quickly, completely and accurately as possible.
   b. Always include when reporting:
      (1) What
      (2) When
      (3) Where
   c. Use the simple, but valid code word, "SALUTE" when reporting.
      Size
      Activity
      Location
      Unit

13.01

Time
Equipment

5. PROCESSING: The turning of information into intelligence by:
      a. Recording.
      b. Evaluation.
      c. Interpretation.

6. Normally information is reported to HQ for processing into intelligence. However, if the procuring agency is isolated, the information is processed at that level for immediate intelligence value.

7. INTELLIGENCE EVALUATION LEGEND.

SOURCES

Report	Means
A	Completely reliable
B	Usually reliable
C	Fairly reliable
D	Not usually reliable
E	Unreliable
F	Reliability unknown

INFORMATION

Report	Means
1	Confirmed by other source
2	Probably true
3	Possibly true
4	Doubtfully true
5	Improbable
6	Truth cannot be judged.

This legend should be applied to intelligence originating in the field and the evaluation sent forward with the information.

8. COUNTERINTELLIGENCE:
    a. Is divided into three general categories.
        (1) Denial
        (2) Detection
        (3) Deception
    b. Counterintelligence at platoon and patrol level.
Consider the use of:
        (1) Sending false messages.
        (2) Phony trails.
        (3) False information.
        (4) Deny civilians access to restricted areas.
    c. Prisoners of war.
        <u>S</u>earch
        <u>S</u>eparate
        <u>S</u>ilence
        <u>S</u>peed
        <u>S</u>afeguard

CHAPTER FOURTEEN

IMMEDIATE ACTION DRILLS

1. GENERAL: Immediate action drills may be defined as prearranged plans for small units predicated upon swift, aggressive action by each member of the unit. Therefore, each soldier must know his duty and be prepared to react instantly in the absence of orders. Normally, these drills, of which there are many, are designed for a particular situation and occur during close-in fighting, i.e., dense woods or jungle. Immediate action drills (IAD) are applicable to conventional and counterguerrilla tactics and may be defensive as well as offensive in nature.

2. FOLLOWING ARE LISTED FOUR COMMON DRILLS.
   a. Freeze:
      (1) Rangers approach trail; point sees enemy first.
      (2) Point signals "freeze" (arm up to rear-palm facing patrol); signal relayed back through patrol.
      (3) All rangers halt and remain motionless to allow enemy to advance as close as possible.
      (4) PL commences firing at opportune moment; no one shoots so long as enemy proceeds to a better position in the "killing zone."
      (5) Any ranger seen by the enemy quickly opens fire.

14.01

b. Hasty Ambush:

(1) Point of ranger patrol sees enemy first; point signals "enemy front" using applicable hand and arm signal. Simultaneously, point or PL must indicate direction for entire patrol, e.g., to the right side of a trail.

(2) Signals quickly relayed back and all move to same side or in direction indicated.

(3) Enemy is allowed to proceed as far as possible into the "killing zone."

(4) PL initiates action - e.g., by firing first, aimed shot.

c. Immediate Assault:

(1) Ranger and enemy sight each other simultaneously.

(2) Point ranger (or whoever is nearest enemy) quickly fires an aimed shot.

(3) . . . then shouts, "Contact, Front!", "Contact, Right!", etc.

(4) Patrol swiftly moves into line and assaults in direction of enemy; moving aggressively and shooting only at seen targets.

(5) PL controls assault until contact is lost or action is finished.

14.02

d. Counter-ambush:
   (1) Part of patrol caught in killing zone.
      (a) Element caught in killing zone must react quickly by returning fire and moving out of this area.
      (b) Those rangers not engaged should assist the group in the killing zone in the quickest manner possible.

   (2) Entire patrol is caught in the killing zone.
      (a) Immediately return fire and move out of killing zone. Use all weapons (smoke is excellent to screen movement).
      (b) If situation permits, mount an attack against the ambush positions using cover and concealment.
      (c) At close quarters, when no cover is available, the only alternative may be to attack directly into the ambush position.

14.03

14.04

CHAPTER FIFTEEN

OPERATIONS ORDER TECHNIQUES

Contents:

PART ONE - THE WARNING ORDER

1. GENERAL: The warning order is to warn the patrol members of an impending mission and to organize their preparation for this mission. The format outlined below covers the information necessary for a warning order. The detail covered in each section is determined by the patrol leader to insure proper coverage.

2. FORMAT:

1. SITUATION:
Brief statement of enemy and friendly situation.

2. MISSION:
State in a clear concise manner and tone. Tailor to fit the patrol; however, keep it as close to the mission given in the briefing as possible.

3. GENERAL INSTRUCTIONS:
   a. General and special organization to include element and team organization and individual duties.
   b. Uniform and equipment common to all, to include identification and camouflage measures.
   c. Weapons, ammunition and equipment each member will carry.
   d. Who will accompany patrol leader on reconnaissance and who will supervise patrol members' preparation during the patrol leader's absence. Also, special tasks for other patrol members to perform. This information may be included in time schedule.
   e. Instructions for obtaining rations, water, weapons, ammunition and equipment.
   f. The chain of command.
   g. A time schedule for the patrol's guidance. Organize it to show When, Where, What, and Who. Include time, place, and uniform for patrol order.

15.02

PART TWO - THE OPERATIONS ORDER FOR A PATROL

1. GENERAL: The operation's order organizes the entire patrol plan into a 5 paragraph format for easy reference and understanding. The format below contains guidance on how to organize your plan to fit this format.

2. FORMAT:

1. SITUATION:
    a. Enemy Forces:
        (1) Weather - Indicate what the weather and light data will be for period of operation and what effects it will have on the patrol.
        (2) Terrain - Indicate the general characteristics of the terrain in the patrol's area of operation.
        (3) Identification - Identify the enemy as to unit.
        (4) Location - State the location of the known or suspected enemy positions.
        (5) Activity - Indicate what the enemy is doing and, if possible, what he is planning to do.
        (6) Strength - State the enemy strength. Indicate what percentage of capability he has.
    b. Friendly Forces:
        (1) Mission of next higher unit - State mission of unit immediately above your unit. If your next higher unit is attached, also indicate the mission of the unit receiving the attachment.
        (2) Locations and planned actions of neighboring units - State the location and missions of the units neighboring your next higher unit. If your next higher unit is attached, give the location and mission of units neighboring the unit receiving the attachment.
        (3) Fire support available for patrol - State the unit designation and type of support (i.e., naval gun, air, artillery) for your patrol. Indicate priority of fires, if applicable.

(4) Mission and routes of other patrols - State the mission and routes of other patrols especially those operating near your patrol. This information is gained through the briefing and through coordination with the other patrols.

  c. Attachments and Detachments: List the patrol attachments and detachments and indicate effective times.

2. MISSION
State the mission in a clear, positive manner and tone. Tailor it to fit the patrol; however, keep it as close to the mission given in the briefing as possible.

3. EXECUTION
  a. Concept of Operation - the overall plan - and missions of elements, teams, and individuals in the objective area. Give a broad explanation or concept of entire plan to get everyone thinking along the same lines. Make it simple and clear.

  b. Other missions, not in the objective area, for elements, teams and individuals. Included are such tasks as navigation, security during movement, and security at halts.

    (1) Elements - State the missions you are giving the elements within your patrol organization.

    (2) Teams - State the missions you are giving the teams within your patrol organization.

    (3) Individuals - State the tasks you are giving individuals within your patrol organization.

  c. Coordinating Instructions:

    (1) Time of departure and return - Normally directed in briefing. If not directed, they may be established by the patrol leader.

    (2) Formations and order of movement - State the initial formation and any known changes, and the internal organization for movement.

    (3) Route - State your route in detail to include terrain features, azimuths and distances. Use training aids for clarity. 15.04

Alternate route of return - Present it as detailed as your route. You may have to use it. Include terrain features, azimuths and distances. Use training aids for clarity.

(4) Passage of friendly positions -

(a) Departure from - State the actions to be taken by the patrol from the time you enter the friendly unit's area through the security halt outside the friendly unit's FEBA.

(b) Re-entry of - Include re-entry procedures from outside the FEBA through the clearing of the friendly unit's area.

(5) Rallying points - Include coordinates and terrain location of the IRP and ORP, tentative rallying points en route may be included. If not included, state you will designate them as you move. Actions at rallying points - Include security considerations, reorganization plan and the period the patrol will remain in the rallying point.

(6) Actions on enemy contact - Plan must include actions to be taken on encountering deliberate ambush and chance contact.

(7) Actions of danger areas - Make a separate plan to cover each type of danger area that may be encountered.

(8) Actions at objective - State actions to be taken by the patrol and positions to be occupied from prior to the leaders' reconnaissance through the withdrawal to the ORP and dissemination of information. Use training aids for clarity.

(9) Fire Support - May be given here; as an annex; or along with route, danger areas, and objective actions.

(10) Rehearsals - Indicate where, when, and what you are going to rehearse. Include priority of items to rehearse and the rehearsal uniform and equipment. Inspections - Indicate where, when, and what you are going to inspect.

15.05

(11) Debriefing - Indicate where, when, and by whom the patrol will be debriefed. State items of special intelligence interest if any have been given you.

4. ADMINISTRATION AND LOGISTICS
   a. Rations - Indicate meals served before departure and after return. If rations are to be carried, indicate what, when and where to pick up rations, if applicable.
   b. Arms and ammunition - Review as stated in warning order. Indicate changes if any.
   c. Uniform and equipment - Review as stated in warning order. Indicate changes if any.
   d. Method of handling wounded - Plan for wounded on way to objective, at the objective, and on return.
   Prisoners - Plan for handling of prisoners taken on way to objective, at the objective, and on return.

5. COMMAND AND SIGNAL
   a. Signal:
   (1) Signals to be used within the patrol - Include hand and arm signals, other signals, codes, and radio call signs.
   (2) Communication with higher headquarters -
   (a) Radio call signs - Include next higher unit, FSC, FL unit and your patrol.
   (b) Primary and alternate frequencies - For all stations you may communicate with.
   (c) Reports - Normally directed in briefing. For example, checkpoints or phase lines.
   (d) Codes - Normally received in briefing. Include any additional code words you have coordinated.
   (3) Challenge and password - Normally received in briefing. Include password to be used forward of FL.
   b. Command:
   (1) Chain of command - Review as stated in warning order. Indicate changes if any.

15.06

(2) <u>Location of patrol leader and assistant in for-</u><u>mation and at the objective</u> - State your location and that of the assistant patrol leader in the order of march for each formation you plan to use.

AIR MOVEMENT ANNEX TO PATROL ORDER

1. SITUATION
   a. Enemy Forces: (To include weather)
   b. Friendly Forces: Unit furnishing support.
   c. Attachments and Detachments.

2. MISSION

3. EXECUTION
   a. Concept of Operation
   b. Missions of Elements, Teams, and Individuals
   c. Organization for Movement
   d. Coordinating Instructions:
      (1) Time aircraft available
      (2) Loading time
      (3) Station time
      (4) Route, landing site, assembly area, alternate plan.
      (5) Serials, flights, and formations
      (6) Action on enemy contact
      (7) Rehearsal

4. ADMINISTRATION AND LOGISTICS
   a. Equipment (may be omitted)
   b. Medical plan (en route and on landing)

5. COMMAND AND SIGNAL
   a. Signal:
      (1) LS marking
      (2) Aircraft release signal
      (3) Call signs/frequencies-alternates.
      (4) Emergency signals
   b. Command:
      (1) Location of PL in air and at destination
      (2) Location of APL in air and at destination
      (3) Location of HQ at destination

15.08

AIR RESUPPLY ANNEX TO PATROL ORDER

1. SITUATION
   a. Enemy Forces: (if it effects the resupply)
   b. Friendly Forces: Unit furnishing support
   c. Attachments and Detachments

2. MISSION

3. EXECUTION
   a. Concept of Operation
   b. Missions of Elements, Teams and Individuals
   c. Coordinating Instructions:
      (1) Location of CCP and heading to drop/landing sites
      (2) Location of RP (may be omitted)
      (3) Location of drop/landing sites
      (4) Marking of drop/landing sites
      (5) Drop altitude (if air drop)
      (6) Drop/land formation
      (7) Landing requirement for aircraft (if landing site)
      (8) Time/date of resupply
      (9) Actions on enemy contact
      (10) Actions at drop/landing sites
      (11) Rehearsal

4. ADMINISTRATION AND LOGISTICS (May be omitted).

5. COMMAND AND SIGNAL
   a. Signal:
      (1) Air to ground call signs and frequencies
      (2) Air drop/air land communication procedure
      (3) Long range visual signal
      (4) Short range visual signal
      (5) Air to ground emergency code
      (6) Obstacle markings

(7) Signals at RP (if applicable)
(8) Code letter at site
(9) Emergency signal for NO DROP/NO LAND

b. Command:
(1) Location of PL
(2) Location of APL
(3) Location of patrol headquarters.

FIRE SUPPORT ANNEX (ARTY) TO PATROL ORDER

1. SITUATION
   a. Enemy Forces: (May be omitted)
   b. Friendly Forces - Unit providing fire support

2. MISSION. (May be omitted)

3. EXECUTION
   a. Preplanned Fires
      (1) Scheduled

	Tgt	Location	TOT	Rd & Fuze
a. Enroute				
b. On obj				

      (2) On-call fires

	Tgt	Location	Rd & Fuze	Code Word
a. Enroute				
b. On obj				

      b. Targets of opportunity
         (1) Communicating procedure
         (2) Method of adjustment

4. ADMINISTRATION AND LOGISTICS. (May be omitted)

5. COMMAND AND SIGNAL
   a. Signal:
      (1) Call signs and frequencies
      (2) Emergency signals
      (3) Code words
   b. Command: (may be omitted)

1 - Appendix - Air Fire Support Plan

15.11

APPENDIX 1 (Air Fire Plan) TO FIRE SUPPORT ANNEX
TO PATROL ORDER

1. SITUATION
   a. Enemy Forces: (may be omitted)
   b. Friendly Forces: Unit providing air support

2. MISSION. (May be omitted)

3. EXECUTION
   a. Preplanned close air support
      (1) Along route

Tgt	Location	TOT	Acft and Armament

      (2) At objective

Tgt	Location	TOT	Acft and Armament

   b. Immediate Support Plan

4. ADMINISTRATION AND LOGISTICS. (May be omitted)

5. COMMAND AND SIGNAL
   a. Signal:
      (1) Call signs and frequencies
      (2) Panel code
      (3) Emergency signals/code words
      (4) Mark target signal
   b. Command: (may be omitted)

PATROL BASE ANNEX TO PATROL ORDER

1. SITUATION. (May be omitted)

2. MISSION

3. EXECUTION
   a. Concept of Operations
   b. Specific Duties of
      (1) Elements
      (2) Teams
      (3) Individuals
   c. Coordinating Instructions:
      (1) Occupation plan
      (2) Operation plan
          (a) Security plan
          (b) Alert plan
          (c) Priority of work
          (d) Evacuation plan

4. ADMINISTRATION AND LOGISTICS
   a. Water Plan
   b. Messing Plan
   c. Hygiene Plan
   d. Maintenance Plan
   e. Rest Plan

5. COMMAND AND SIGNAL
   a. Signals:
      (1) Call signs and frequencies
      (2) Code words
      (3) Emergency signals
   b. Command:
      (1) Location of patrol leader
      (2) Location of assistant patrol leader
      (3) Location of patrol headquarters

STREAM CROSSING ANNEX TO PATROL ORDER

1. SITUATION
   a. Enemy Forces:
      (1) Weather
      (2) Terrain
         (a) River width
         (b) River depth
         (c) Current
         (d) Vegetation
         (e) Obstacles
      (3) Enemy location, identification, activity
   b. Friendly Forces:

2. MISSION

3. EXECUTION
   a. Concept of Operation
   b. Missions:
      (1) Elements
      (2) Teams
      (3) Individuals
   c. Coordinating Instructions:
      (1) Crossing procedure
      (2) Security
      (3) Order of crossing
      (4) Actions on enemy contact
      (5) Alternate plan
      (6) Rallying points
      (7) Rehearsal plan

4. ADMINISTRATION AND LOGISTICS. (May be omitted)

5. COMMAND AND SIGNAL
   a. Signal: (May be omitted)
   b. Command:
      (1) Location of PL

15.14

(2) Location of APL
(3) Location of HQ

SMALL BOAT ANNEX TO PATROL ORDER

1. SITUATION
   a. Enemy Forces:
      (1) Weather
          (a) Tide
          (b) Surf
          (c) Wind
      (2) Terrain
      (3) Identification, location, activity and strength
   b. Friendly Forces: Unit furnishing support, if applicable.
   c. Attachments and Detachments: (May be omitted)

2. MISSION

3. EXECUTION
   a. Concept of Operation
   b. Organization for Movement
   c. Missions of Elements, Teams and Individuals
      (1) Security teams
      (2) Tie-down teams
          (a) Load equipment
          (b) Secure equipment
      (3) Designation of cox-swains/boat commanders
      (4) Selection of navigator(s) and observer(s)
   d. Coordinating Instructions:
      (1) Formations and order of movement
      (2) Route and alternate route of return
      (3) Method of navigation
      (4) Actions on enemy contact
      (5) Embarkation plan
      (6) Debarkation plan
      (7) Rehearsals

4. ADMINISTRATION AND LOGITICS
   a. Rations (may be omitted)
15.16

b. Arms and Ammunition (may be omitted)

c. Uniform and Equipment

    (1) Method of distribution of paddles and life jackets

    (2) Disposition of boat, paddles and life jackets upon debarkation

d. Method of handling wounded and prisoners (may be omitted)

5. COMMAND AND SIGNAL

    a. Signal:

        (1) Signals to be used between and in boats

        (2) Code words

    b. Command:

        (1) Location of patrol leader

        (2) Location of assistant patrol leader

PART FOUR - THE PLATOON OPERATION ORDER

1. The following information is extracted from appropriate field manuals, as indicated.

2. (From FM 7-15, Rifle Platoons and Squads--Infantry, Airborne, and Mechanized, 1965, para .10):

"Operation Order: An operation order sets forth the organization for combat (task organization), the situation, the mission, the commander's decision and plan of action, and the details of execution needed to insure coordinated action by a unit. The order format and content is discussed in appendix II, FM 7-11."
(From FM 7-11, Rifle Company--Infantry, Airborne, and Mechanized, 1965, Appendix II, Section II):

Format for Operation Orders

"Task Organizations:
The task organization establishes the internal organization for combat of the company for an operation. It includes all organic and attached combat support elements, as well as those placed in direct support of the company. In a written order ....(omitted). Use of the task organization, particularly in oral orders, shortens the company commander's order, expedites its issuance, and facilitates ready understanding of instructions by subordinates. In the issuance of oral orders, if there are no attachments to, or detachments from, the company and no attachments are to be made to the platoons, the task organization need not be mentioned. If the order involves a continuation of a tactical operation, and no changes are to be made in the existing organization for combat, the commander would state: "No change in task organization." On the other hand, if there are changes to the task organization, the company commander would mention only the changes; he
15.18

need not mention all units. When the task organization is used, the attachments to, and the detachments from, the company, or attachments to the platoons, need not be repeated in sub-paragraph 1c or paragraph 3 of the order.

"1. SITUATION
This paragraph contains information of the enemy and friendly forces that subordinates should know in order to accomplish their missions. Only pertinent information is included. When the order being prepared represents a continuation of a current tactical operation and elements normally shown in paragraph 1 have not changed from the preceding order or known situation, it is permissible for the sake of brevity to so indicate, or to cite only those items which have changed. (For example: 'Enemy forces: No change.' 'Artillery and Engineer support remains unchanged.')·

a. Enemy Forces: Information of the enemy pertaining to the operation, such as locations, dispositions, strength, activities, and capabilities.

b. Friendly Forces: Mission of next higher unit, location and missions of adjacent units, and missions of non-organic supporting elements which may affect the actions of the unit.

c. Attachments and Detachments: Elements attached to, or detached from, the unit for the operation, including the effective time of attachment or detachment.

"2. MISSION
A clear, concise statement of the task to be accomplished by the unit.

"3. EXECUTION
This paragraph states the tactical plan for the conduct of the operation and assigns specific missions to each subordinate combat element, including attachments.

a. Concept of Operation: In the concept of operation,

15.19

the commander states his scheme of maneuver--as derived from his estimate of the situation (his decision)--and his use of fire support for the operation. Full use of "concept of operation," together with graphic control measures and/or terrain orientation, are used to convey the tactical concept and missions of major maneuver units. This technique permits mentioning units in order of importance to the role they are to play, without regard to numerical designation; e.g., in an attack situation, the platoon making the main attack is mentioned first, followed by supporting attack(s), then the reserve. Thus, in oral orders, subordinates may grasp readily the overall scheme of maneuver while at the same time receive their specific missions or instructions. When missions for the maneuver units are clearly stated in the "concept of operation", they need not be repeated in the subparagraph for that unit.

b. Unit missions or tasks not stated in the "concept of operation" may be specified to units concerned after the concept is stated. These would include contingency or "be prepared" instructions to the maneuver units, as appropriate, and missions for the combat support units. In assigning an element its mission, attachments or detachments are indicated, unless specified in the task organization.

c. The final subparagraph of paragraph 3 is entitled "Coordinating Instructions" and contains tactical instructions and details of coordination and control applicable to two or more units (For example: line of departure, final coordination line, boundaries, provisions for troop safety, control measures for assault, or restrictions.) Full use of this subparagraph, together with the task organization and paragraph 3a, will expedite issuance of oral orders and facilitate understanding on the part of recipients.

"4. ADMINISTRATION AND LOGISTICS
This paragraph contains information or instructions pertaining to rations, ammunition, location of distributing points, company trains, medical support, and prisoner-of-

15.20

war collecting point, transportation, and other administra
tive and supply matters. Only necessary information is
included.

"5. COMMAND AND SIGNAL
a. Special signal instructions, which include such
items as prearranged signals and restrictions on the use
of radio or other means of communications.
b. Location of the commander and command post
during the operation."

3. The foregoing extracts represent official Army
doctrine on the operation order at platoon and squad level
While they are written specifically for company-level
orders, the well-trained platoon or squad leader must be
capable of using this general format to organize his plan
for any type of operation into clear, logical form. It will
be noted that the patrol order formats contained in Parts
Two and Three of this chapter are detailed applications of
this same general format to small-unit patrolling operations in a conventional warfare situation. The use of annexes to cover aspects of the operation which require detailed instructions is advisable whenever the order can
thereby be made more clear and concise.

CHAPTER SIXTEEN

PASSAGE OF THE FORWARD UNIT

DEPARTURE THROUGH FORWARD UNIT

1. Patrol detrucks. (patrol may move into an assembly area or may move into Initial Rallying Point (IRP)).

2. Patrol Ldr and party complete final coordination with front line comdr or his representative at Command Post (CP).

3. Patrol moves to a closer covered and concealed position to the passage point (initial rally point). Guide leads clearing party to the passage point.

4. Security party clears the area forward of the front line to the limit of the unit's Final Protective Fires.

5. After area is cleared patrol moves forward to the passage point.

6. The patrol is counted through the passage point by the APL.

7. Patrol moves quickly and silently through the final protective fire zone without stopping.

8. A security halt is executed after the patrol has cleared the final protective fire zone.

9. Patrol moves out on way to objective.

RE-ENTRY THROUGH FORWARD UNIT

1. Halt patrol outside final protective fire zone and contact FLU.

2. Reconnaissance team probes for re-entry point.

3. Re-entry point is located and contact with guide is established.

4. The patrol moves forward to the re-entry point.

5. Each patrol member is identified and counted through the re-entry point by the APL.

6. Guide from front line guides patrol to vicinity of CP and IRP as appropriate.

7. Patrol Ldr renders spot report to Comdr on status of patrol and any information that is of immediate value to the front line unit.

8. The patrol departs area as quickly as security permits and returns to parent unit for debriefing.

CHAPTER SEVENTEEN

PATROL BASE DRILL

1. LOCAL SECURITY: Halt patrol 200-400 meters from patrol base site. Patrol establishes local security. Patrol members take several steps to right or left, distributing themselves evenly to either side of the line of march. Early warning is put out a short distance (approximately 50 meters) from the flanks and rear security drops back approximately the same distance. The point team provides early warning 50 meters to the front of the patrol. Element leaders move to the head of their elements. APL moves to the head of the patrol.

2. PATROL BASE RECON: Patrol leader informs the APL that he is about to recon the tentative patrol base site and names the individuals who will assist in this task - suggested number is four people other than the patrol leader. One member of the recon party should be an RTO. The APL is further instructed concerning the action he is to take if either the recon party or the main body minus is hit while the two are separated. The patrol leader, with his recon party, recons the tentative patrol base site to insure its suitability and security. If the site is found suitable, two men are dispatched from the site to pick up the main body of the patrol and bring them in. Among the three individuals remaining at the site to keep it under surveillance is the RTO.

3. OCCUPATION: Patrol moves to the patrol base site in some manner which will confuse a pursuing enemy as to the alignment of the route taken into the base. A tentative OP is positioned at a point from which the enemy's attempts to follow any trail sign left by the patrol may be

observed. The patrol enters the base from some point
other than 6 o'clock. Rear security camouflages the entry
point and obliterates trail signs immediately adjacent to it.
The patrol leader is positioned at the center of the base.
Element leaders move directly to the patrol leader and file
out to perimeter along the left flank of sectors assigned by
the clock system. Elements occupy the perimeter by moving clockwise. A small patrol may find it expedient to occupy a patrol base perimeter merely by moving in a circle,
with the patrol leader at the head of the file, from the point
of entry.

    4. PERIMETER ADJUSTMENT: Patrol leader moves
to first element leader and with him checks perimeter in
clockwise direction. Each element leader meets the patrol
leader at the left flank of his sector.

    5. AREA RECON: R & S teams (ideally consisting of
two men - one of whom might appropriately be the element
leader whose sector front the team is to recon) depart from
the left flank of the element and move on designated azimuth and distance from the base. R& S teams search for
indications of enemy or civilians, suitable OP's and LP's,
rally points, and withdrawal routes, R & S teams return to
the right flank of their elements and report to the element
leader if he is not already a member of the team. Element leaders report to the patrol leader. The patrol leader
determines rally points, OP's, and routes of withdrawal.

    6. EMPLACEMENT OF OP/LP'S: OP/LP's are
placed into position under the personal supervision of one
of the patrols principal leaders. Commo with OP/LP's is
co-ordinated. OP/LP's are carefully instructed concerning actions they are to take if the patrol base is attacked or
rapidly evacuated for any reason. OP's should consist of
two personnel if the size of the patrol and number of OP's

permit this. One man OP's must be relieved regularly. OP's become LP's at night and should shift positions slightly at night. The PL may be appraised of new LP locations by using the old location as a reference point and shifting from it. A squad-size patrol or smaller will normally pull their OP's in at night and go into a tight wagon wheel perimeter.

7. ORGANIZATION OF THE PATROL BASE: Organization of a patrol base is continuous and includes: Planning base defenses; confinement of noise making to specific periods; adhering to the priority of work (such as preparing positions, maintenance, hygiene, eating, rest), selecting water points, digging refuse pits, rehearsing stand-to and evacuation, and planning.

CHAPTER EIGHTEEN

COMMUNICATIONS

CHARACTERISTICS OF RADIOS

1. CALIBRATING RANGE.
   a. AN/PRC-25 High band
      53-75.95
      Low band
      30-52.95
   b. AN/PRT-4 (transmitter) 47.0-57.0. AN/PRR-9 (receiver) 47.0-57.0.

2. STEPS IN OPERATING.
   a. AN/PRC-25
      (1) Turn function switch to ON position.
      (2) Set the band switch at 30-52 or 53-75 depending on channel used.
      (3) Turn tuning control so the desired channel shows on the channel dial.
      (4) Set the volume control at 4 and contact distant station.
   b. AN/PRT-4 (transmitter).
      (1) Insert battery insuring battery retainer is securely clasped.
      (2) Extend collapsible antenna fully.
      (3) Place channel selector switch in desired position; CH-1 or CH-2.
      (4) Tone-Voice lockout tab in center detent position gives both voice and tone communication.
         (a) For voice transmission, press and hold TONE-Voice switch in direction of TONE arrow.
         (b) For Tone transmission, press and hold TONE-VOICE switch in direction of Tone arrow.

c. AN/PRR-9 (Receiver).

(1) Insure power switch is in OFF position.

(2) Insert battery through battery clip.

(3) Loosen antenna thumb screw, rotate antenna upright and retighten thumb screw.

(4) For receiving with squelch, rotate receiver control clockwise to its mid-position or until a comfortable listening level is obtained.

(5) For receiving without squelch rotate receiver control fully clockwise then rotate counterclockwise until a comfortable listening level is obtained.

3. OPERATING RANGE:

    a. AN/PRC-25   5-8 km.
    b. AN/PRT-4 Ch-1   1-5K
              Ch-2   500M

4. RADIO PROCEDURE.

    a. Phonetic alphabet:

A-alpha	J-juliet	S-sierra
B-bravo	K-kilo	T-tango
C-charlie	L-lima	U-uniform
D-delta	M-mike	V-victor
E-echo	N-november	W-whiskey
F-foxtrot	O-oscar	X-x-ray
G-golf	P-papa	Y-yankee
H-hotel	Q-quebec	Z-zulu
I-india	R-romeo	

b.

Prowords	Definition
this is	this transmission is from station whose designation follows.
over	this is the end of my transmission and a response is necessary.
out	this is the end of my transmission no answer is required.
roger	I have received your transmission satisfactory.
say again	repeat all of last transmission.
correction	an error has been made in this transmission.
message follows	a message that require recording follows.
wilco	I have received your message, understand it, and will comply.

Prowords	Definition
I say again	I am repeating transmission or portion indicated.
break	I hereby indicate the separation of the text from other portions of the message.

5. EXPEDIENT ANTENNA.
    a. Types.
       (1) Suspended vertical antenna.
       (2) Half rhombic antenna.
       (3) Long wire antenna.
    b. Antenna length. It is important to have correct antenna length when operating on a given frequency.

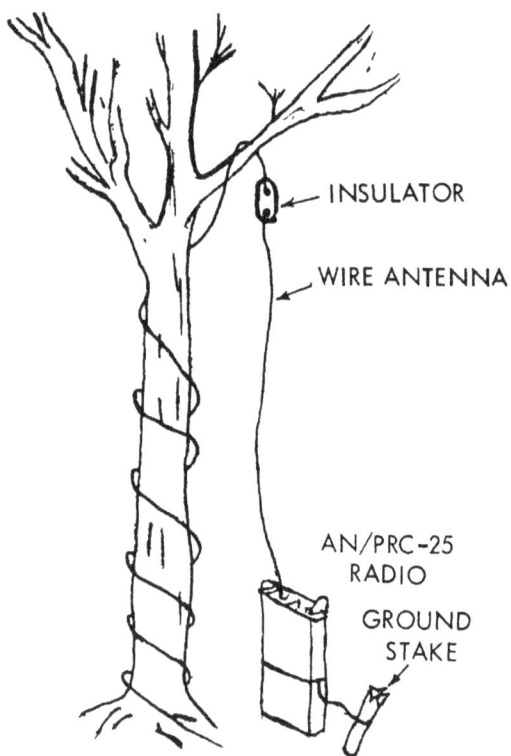

INSULATOR

WIRE ANTENNA

AN/PRC-25
RADIO

GROUND
STAKE

18.04

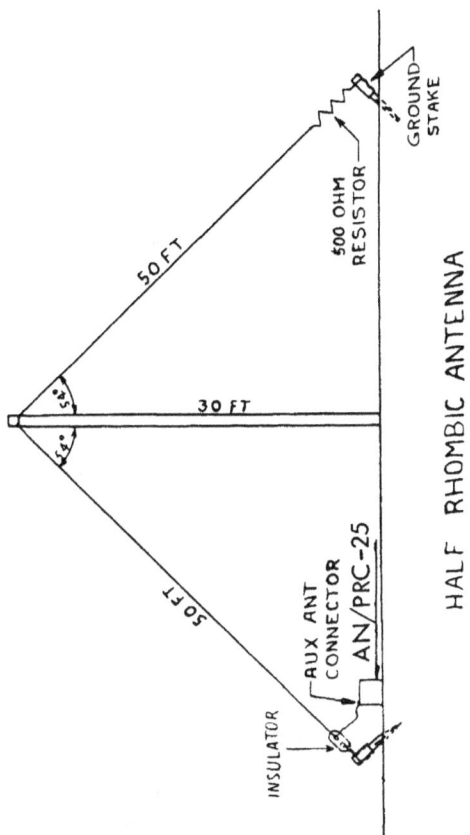

HALF RHOMBIC ANTENNA

50 FT

30 FT

50 FT

500 OHM
RESISTOR

GROUND
STAKE

AUX ANT
CONNECTOR

AN/PRC-25

INSULATOR

18.05

VERTICAL POLARIZATION 20 TO
80 MC.

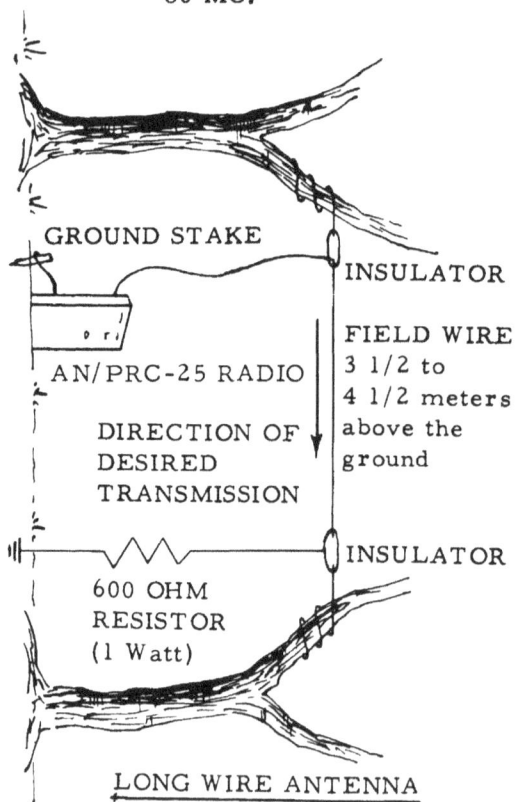

GROUND STAKE

INSULATOR

AN/PRC-25 RADIO

FIELD WIRE
3 1/2 to
4 1/2 meters
above the
ground

DIRECTION OF
DESIRED
TRANSMISSION

INSULATOR

600 OHM
RESISTOR
(1 Watt)

LONG WIRE ANTENNA

18.06

CHAPTER NINETEEN

PATROL ROUTES

1. GENERAL CONSIDERATIONS.
   a. Mission.
   b. Cover and concealment.
   c. Man made and natural obstacles.
   d. Enemy locations.

2. ROUTE SELECTION.
   a. Make a thorough terrain analysis.
   b. Compare possible routes considering.
      (1) Mission.
          (a) Type patrol.
          (b) Size.
          (c) Time limitations.
      (2) Cover and concealment.
          (a) Terrain and vegetation.
          (b) Weather and light data.
      (3) Obstacles.
          (a) Avoid man made obstacles.
          (b) Consider use of natural obstacles.
          (c) Consider time to negotiate.
      (4) Enemy locations.
   c. Select the best route based on above considerations.

3. NAVIGATIONAL PLANNING.
   a. Direction.
      (1) General azimuth (terrain and compass).
      (2) Dead reckoning (compass only).
      (3) Consider:
          (a) Offset technique.
          (b) Box-in technique.
      (4) Use check points.

19. 01

b. Distance
    (1) Divide route into short legs (600 to 1000 M)
    (2) Terminate legs at checkpoints.
    (3) Pace each leg separately.
    (4) Use checkpoints.

4. DIFFERENT RETURN ROUTE.
    a. Apply same tactical and navigational considera-tions.
    b. Select so movement cannot be seen or heard from approach route.
    c. Plan for a different re-entry point into friendly lines.

CHAPTER TWENTY

SURVIVAL

1. GENERAL: Finding yourself isolated behind enemy lines, in a desolate area, or in enemy hands, can be eased or even avoided if you remember the key word: S-U-R-V-I-V-A-L,

S--Size up the situation by considering yourself, the country and the enemy.

U--Undue haste makes waste.
    a. Don't be too eager to move.
    b. Don't lose your temper.
    c. Face the facts--danger exists.

R--Remember where you are.

V--Vanquish fear and panic.
    a. To feel fear is normal.
    b. When you are injured, it is difficult to control fear.
    c. Panic can be caused by loneliness.
    d. Planning your escape will help keep your mind busy.

I--Improving.
    a. You can always improve the situation.
    b. Learn to put up with new and unpleasant conditions.

V--Value living.
    a. Hope, and a real plan for escape, reduces your fear and makes your chances of survival better,
    b. Conserve your health and strength.
    c. Hunger, cold and fatigue lower your efficiency and stamina.
    d. Remember your goal - getting out alive.

A--Act like the natives.

L--Learn basic skills.

2. PLANT FOOD: There are at least 300,000 different kinds of wild plants in the world. A large number of them are potentially edible, although some are more tasty and palatable than others.

Edibility Rules. Never eat large quantities of a strange food without first testing it. Prepare a cooked sample, then take a mouthful, chew it, and hold it in your mouth for 5 minutes. If it still tastes good, go ahead and eat it. If the taste is disagreeable, don't eat it. A burning, nauseating, or bitter taste is a warning of danger. In gen eral, it is safe to try foods that you observe being eaten by birds and mammals. Avoid eating plants with milky joice. Avoid eating plants that taste disagreeable (bitterness is a guide).

3. ANIMAL FOOD: Animal food will give you the most food value per pound. Anything that creeps, crawls, swims, or flies is a possible source of food.

   a. Butchering and skinning: Skin large game; bleed and gut all animals. You can drink small amounts of blood, but you should throw away the intestines. Use care in removing gall and urine bladders; if they are broken, the meat will be tainted. Washing will help clean your meat.

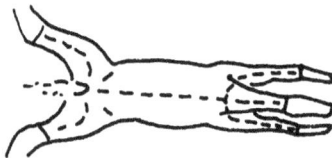

NOTE:
Cut as
shown.

b. Traps and snares: Indiscriminate placing of traps in a waste of time. Small game such as rabbits, mice, etc., travel on paths through the vegetation. Set traps in or over these trails. Fish hooks can be made from items with points or pins, such as nail files, collar insignia and campaign ribbons; or from bird bones, fish spines, and pieces of wood.

    (1) Dead fall with fire 4 trigger.

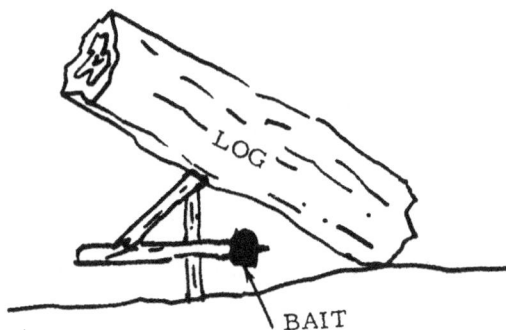

    (2) Small animal "twitch-up."

SENSITIVE
TRIGGER

4. FOOD PREPARATION:
a. Cooking: Hot meals are beneficial to morale
and proper heating kills many germs. Boiling, roasting,
baking, and frying, in order of preference, are efficient ways of preparing foods. Boiling is the best method
as it preserves the natural juices of the food.
b. Preserving foods: In cold climates, preserve
your excess foods by freezing. Plant food can be dried by
wind, sun, air, or fire, or any combination of these four.
Meat can be made into "Jerky" by cutting it across the
grain in one-fourth inch strips and either drying it in the
sun or by smoking it.
c. Fires: Fires should be made in a depression
in the ground during the hottest part of the day when the
air is driest. The area should have concealment from

20.04

long range observation. Hill tops and low ground should be avoided. Dry hardwood burns slower, gives off more heat, and produces less smoke than other types.

5. WATER: Water will be one of your first and most important needs. Start looking for it immediately. You can get along for weeks without food, but you can't live long without water, especially in hot areas where you lose large quantities of water through sweating.

a. Purification: Purify all water before drinking, either (1) by boiling for at least one minute; or (2) by using the water purification tablets; or (3) by adding 8 drops of 2 1/2% solution of iodine to a quart (canteenful) of water and letting it stand for 10 minutes before drinking. Rainwater collected directly in clean containers or in plants is generally safe to drink without purifying. Don't drink urine or sea water - the salt content is too high.

b. Survival water still: Described below is a cheap and simple survival still that will produce drinking water even in a dry desert.

(1) Basic materials for setting up this still are: (1) 6x6 foot sheet of clean plastic; (2) a container, 2 to 4 qt capacity; (3) 5 ft flexible plastic tubing.

(2) Once you've picked a likely unshaded spot for the still, cig the hole. If you have no shovel, you can use a stick or even your hands. The hole should be about three feet across. Maintain this diameter for a few inches down and then slope the hole toward the bottom, as shown in the accompanying diagram. The hole should be deep enough so that the point of the plastic cone can be about 18 inches below ground and still clear the top of the bucket. With the hole properly dug, tape one end of the plastic drinking tube inside the bucket, and set the bucket dead center in the bottom of the hole. Run the other end of the drinking tube up and out of the hole. Being careful to leave the top end of the drinking tube free, lay the plastic sheet

20. 05

over the hole and pile enough dirt around the edge to hold
it securely. Use a fist-size rock to weight down the center of the plastic, and make any adjustments necessary to
bring it within a couple of inches of the top of the bucket.

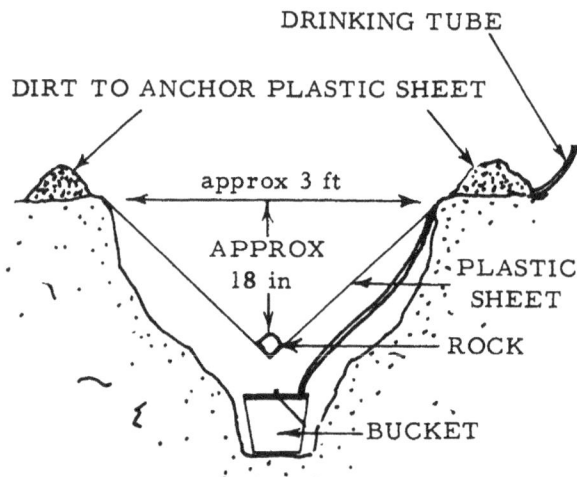

DRINKING TUBE

DIRT TO ANCHOR PLASTIC SHEET

approx 3 ft

APPROX
18 in

PLASTIC
SHEET

ROCK

BUCKET

NOTE: Cross-section of survival still. Heat from sun
vaporizes ground water. Then this vapor con-
denses under plastic, trickles down, drops into
bucket.

  6. SHELTERS: The kind of shelter you make depends
on whether you need protection from rain, cold, heat, sun-
shine or insects, and also whether your camp is only for a
night or for many days. Pick the location for your camp
carefully. Try to be near fuel and water-especially water.
Don't make camp at the base of steep slopes or in areas
where you run the risk of avalances, floods, rockfalls or
battering by winds.

20.06

PONCHO SHELTERS

7. NAVIGATION: In a survival situation you may well find yourself without a compass. The ability to determine direction may enable you to navigate yourself back to your unit or to a friendly sanctuary. Some methods of direction determination are:

a. You can use the sun to find approximate true north. This method can be used anytime the sun is bright enough for a stick placed in the ground to cast a shadow. Find a fairly straight stick about three feet long and follow these steps.

(1) Push the stick into the ground at a level spot so that it is straight up and down.

(2) Mark the tip of the shadow with a small rock and wait until the shadow moves a few inches (10 to 15 minutes).

(3) Mark the tip of the second shadow.

(4) Draw a line from the first rock to the second rock and about a foot past the second rock.

(5) Stand with the toe of your left foot at the first rock, and the toe of your right foot at the end of the line you draw. You are now facing north.

b. Another method which may be used if you should have a watch is to divide the time of day by two (using military time) take the answer number and point it toward the sun. You will have the N-S line running from 12 to 6.

EXAMPLE: Time 1800. Divide by 2 is nine, pointed toward sun. N-S line from 12 to 6.

c. Finding directions by night, look for the Big Dipper. The two stars at the end of the bowl are called the pointer. In a straight line out from the pointer is the North Star (at about five times the distance between the pointers). The Big Dipper rotates slowly around the North Star and does not always appear in the same position.

CHAPTER TWENTY-ONE

WEAPONS

Weapon	Weight	Max Eff Range	Basic Load*
.45 cal pistol	2.5 lbs	50 m.	21 rounds
M14 rifle	10.2 lbs	460 m.	100 rounds
M14A1	13 lbs	460 m.	260 rounds
M14E2 rifle	14.5 lbs	460 m. (700 m. for semi-automatic fire)	260 rounds
M60 machinegun	23 lbs	1,100 m.	2200 rounds
M16A1 rifle	7.6 lbs	460 m.	140 rounds
M79 grenade launcher	6.5 lbs	150 m. (300 m. for area fire)	18 rounds
M72 light anti-tank weapon	4.5 lbs	230 m.	Unit 50 P per man

GRENADES

Type	Casualty Radius
Fragmentation, M26A2 (Hand)	15 meters
WP, M34 (Hand)	25 meters
M79 HE round	5 meters

CHAPTER TWENTY-TWO

CONVOY MOVEMENT

1. PRECAUTIONS: Move along dangerous roads only in convoy (two or more vehicles) - best to move during day light.

    a. Full use of armored vehicles.

    b. Other vehicles move at intervals of at least 100m.

    c. SOP's must include:

      (1) Appoint convoy and vehicle commanders - issue specific orders.

      (2) Organization of convoy.

      (3) Weapons to be carried plus ammo. Include AR's, LMG's, M-79's, etc.

      (4) Instructions regarding vehicles i.e., canvas, sides, bows, tailgates, sandbags and windshields.

      (5) Immediate action drills established.

      (6) Communications and signals within convoy and coordinated actions along route, i.e., patrol's ETA at certain points.

      (7) Fire support coordination.

      (8) Coordination with units you are passing through.

      (9) Communications with next higher unit.

    d. All drivers and men must be briefed to include maintaining contact, speeds, route, number of men per vehicle, duties of sentries and action to be taken if ambushed.

    e. Along especially dangerous routes: All men must remain alert at all times and ready for action. Prior to entry into a likely area for ambush, troops should dismount and scout flanks ahead while part of the convoy covers their movement. The unit can then move by bounds through this area.

22.01

f. Preparation and loading vehicles:

(1) Trucks should have canvas and bows removed, sides off, windshield down benches, equipment or sandbags placed in center of cargo area to allow men to face in outward position. Sandbags in floor of cab and rear cargo area - also along sides for some protection against mines.

(2) Sixteen to seventeen men is maximum number that can be safely carried in 2 1/2 ton truck. Make certain all men can move and shoot without being overcrowded.

g. The vehicle commander is responsible for keeping his men alert, maintaining contact by controlling the driver, and commanding his men in event of ambush. His position is in rear of vehicle. Designate an assistant vehicle commander.

h. Lookout sentries: Four men, one in each corner of vehicle, who are armed preferably with automatic weapons. During long trips these men are rotated because of fatigue caused by constantly scanning the road. Lookout nearest driver assists vehicle commander in maintaining contact with preceding vehicle.

i. Smoke sentries: Two men designated grenadier, one facing left and one right. They are preferably armed with WP smoke grenades. Grenades are held ready for quick throwing in event vehicle is forced to stop in the killing zone (KZ).

j. Other weapons: LMG's can be mounted by improvised attachment, provided the gun can be quickly removed. Light mortars: Usually there is overhead clearance along road and weapon can be used in vehicle or along road while troops maneuver to ambush flank or rear. M-79's or rifle grenades: Used similar to mortar. WP smoke: Extremely effective. Creates an immediate smoke screen; phosphorous can cause casualties. Also use H.C. smoke grenades for concealment.

22.02

k. Tactics: Aircraft, both tactical and recon, should be used if available, to scout for likely ambush sites. Never establish patterns in road movement. Maintain secrecy when planning times and routes. Armor can be used as an advance guard, and in the rear of the convoy. If ambush occurs, armor can drive forward into ambush rather than turning around or traversing guns to rear.

2. ACTION ON CONTACT: Basic principle is never to halt in KZ. Vehicles caught in the KZ should try to increase speed and drive through this area, stopping only when out of KZ or before moving in to it. Then, attack immediately from flanks and rear.

a. When no troops have entered KZ: Convoy commander, or 2d in command, must commence an immediate flank attack, using any support available such as LMG's, artillery, tactical air.

b. When all troops are clear ahead of KZ: Similar to paragraph 2.a. above, and a flank attack must be launched as soon as vehicles can be stopped and men readied.

c. When troops are on near and far sides of KZ: Confusion may result and time lost deciding which group mounts the attack - also inter-unit clash may take place. As general rule, group which has not entered KZ should mount a flank attack as in paragraph 2.a. above. Group on far side might circle to rear of ambush to intercept or ambush enemy force.

d. When troops are forced to stop within KZ:

(1) Lookout sentries immediately commence firing, while all other troops detruck and move in direction indicated by vehicle commander. He may order "MOVE RIGHT" or "MOVE LEFT." Get off vehicle as quickly as possible using both sides and rear. Then move in direction designated.

(2) Simultaneously, grenadiers throw WP or HC smoke to cover troops detrucking.

22.03

(3) After all troops clear the vehicle, the look-out sentries detruck and join in the action.

(4) All troops must now begin immediate counter-action. Wounded must be left until after the battle Primary concern is to get out of KZ as quickly as possible. Move fast; return fire. Use smoke; leaders retain control. Use available cover when moving out of KZ. Commander must then decide whether to set up perimeter defense or continue the attack. Often, in open country, a determined and immediate assault on the ambush position may be the only solution for escape. Before departure, rehearse drills until proficient.

(5) Consider driving the vehicle off of the road pointed in direction of main ambush. This should provide a few seconds temporary cover for troops while they off load. It also points out the direction of the main force for any air cover on station.

(6) In the event a successful assault cannot be mounted and the element cannot move out of the KZ, establish a strong perimeter and deliver maximum fire to gain fire superiority. Immediately call for artillery and other support.

22.04

CHAPTER TWENTY-THREE

HELICOPTER RAPPELLING

1. PURPOSE OF HELICOPTER RAPPELLING: To deliver men and equipment from a helicopter to the ground when the ground configuration, vegetation, and other factors do not allow landing.

2. KEY POINTS OF RAPPELLING TRAINING: The following points are the highlights of helicopter rappelling training. It is emphasized that the training is unique and technique and instruction are derived mainly from experience and common sense with a high priority on safety standards.

    a. Practical work in ropes and knots:

        (1) Type ropes used:

            (a) Two (2) 120' rappel ropes, nylon, 7/16" diameter.

            (b) One (1) 12' sling rope, 1/2" Manila or nylon.

        (2) Type knots used:

            (a) Square knot - used in swiss seat.

            (b) Round turn w/two half hitches, the clove hitch, and the bowline - used as anchor knots.

            (c) Bowline on a coil - used in the chest harness.

    b. Equipment used during the conduct of helicopter rappelling:

        (1) Individual rappellers equipment:

            (a) Steel helmet w/chin strap (airborne type liner).

            (b) Gloves, leather, work w/liners.

            (c) Rappel ring, one (1) each.

            (d) Snap link, one (1) each.

            (e) Plastic goggles.

(f) Sling rope, 12' Manila hemp or nylon.

(g) Two (2) 120' nylon rappelling ropes.

(2) The rappelling kit for a UH-1D helicopter:

(a) DONUT ring consists of:

1. 120" steel cable, 1/2" diameter.

2. Four (4) U-bolt clamps.

3. Seven (7) static line snap fasteners.

4. One (1) 12" keeper chain.

5. One (1) rappel ring (floating safety ring).

(3) Other equipment used:

(a) Rope coiling log (2-3" diameter, 1-1/4' to 2' long).

(b) Ground helicopter mock-ups (simulates struts of UH-1D helicopter).

(c) Rappelling towers, 15' above ground.

c. Ground mock-up training.

(1) Rappeller attaching himself to the rappelling rope.

(a) The rappel rope is looped through the rappel ring.

(b) The snap link w/gate down is attached to the rappel ring and the swiss seat.

(c) The snap link and the rappel ring are taped together to preclude movement.

(2) The use of the basic principle of rappelling - FRICTION.

(a) Two (2) loops through the rappel ring is most desirable method of hook-up.

(b) The rappeller decends down the rope at a speed determined by the amount of pressure exerted by his BRAKE HAND.

(c) CAUTION: The two (2) loops must always be taken from the slack between the rappeller and his anchor point.

(3) The use of the "L" position:

(a) Legs parallel to the ground.

23. 02

(b) Upper portion of the body bent slightly forward at the waist.

(c) The right hand (BRAKE HAND) grasps running end of rope and is positioned in the small of the back.

(d) The left hand holds the standing end of the rope well above the RAPPEL RING. The left hand is used strictly for balance and guidance.

    d. Conduct of tower training.

      (1) Commands for tower exits:

        (a) "HOOK UP".

          1. Rappeller attaches self to rappelling ropes.

          2. Rappeller attaches rappelling ropes to DONUT RING and then to. FLOATING SAFETY RING.

          3. Rappeller prepares slack between DONUT RING and himself and sits on edge of tower.

        (b) "CHECK EQUIPMENT".

          1. Rappeller looks toward DONUT RING and pulls rope to check secureness.

          2. Rappeller checks RAPPEL SEAT.

          3. Rappeller checks RAPPEL RING to insure rope is inserted properly.

          4. Rappeller reports "EQUIPMENT CHECKED" and puts BRAKE HAND in position behind buttocks.

        (c) "POSITION". Rappeller assumes "L" position on simulated skid and gives command "READY TO GO".

        (d) "GO" (This command is given by the instructor after he has made the necessary final checks).

          1. The rappeller flexes his knees and "Crow Hops" away from the tower releasing pressure on the BRAKE HAND and exits the tower.

          2. Rappeller makes an initial stop after descending 5-10 ft.

        3. During descent, the rappeller maintains the "L" position.

        4. When reaching the ground and removing the ropes from the RAPPEL RING, the rappeller yells "OFF RAPPEL" and moves quickly away from the tower.

    e. Conduct of live helicopter rappelling.

      (1) Rappellers familiarization with the configuration of the aircraft.

        (a) Safety procedures.

        (b) DONUT RING preparation.

        (c) Check of all TIE-DOWNS.

        (d) Procedures for HOOK UP.

        (e) Sealing and positioning of ropes (RAPPELLING) in the aircraft.

        (f) Positioning of ROPE COILING LOGS in the aircraft.

      (2) Positioning in Acft:

        (a) When flight time to rappelling site is more than five (5) minutes.

        1. Rappellers are seated on floor near door with legs inside aircraft.

        2. The forward seated rappellers face rearward and the rear seated rappellers face forward.

        (b) When flight time to rappelling site is less than five (5) minutes:

        1. Rappellers are seated in the door facing outward with feet hanging out toward skid bar.

        2. All rappellers are completely hooked up and safety checked prior to leaving ground.

        3. While in the helicopter, all rappellers will have BRAKE HAND in position with no slack between brake hand and DONUT RING.

      (3) Commands and Procedures for aircraft exit.

        (a) "CHECK EQUIPMENT".

         1. Rappeller looks toward DONUT RING and pulls on rope to check secureness.

         2. Rappeller checks RAPPEL SEAT.

         3. Rappeller checks RAPPEL RING to insure rope is inserted properly.

         4. Rappeller reports "EQUIPMENT CHECKED" and puts brake hand on.

    (d) "IN THE DOOR". The rappeller assumes position seated in the door with feet hanging out towards skid.

    (c) "ON THE STRUT".

         1. The rappeller uses guide hand and anchor end of rope to assist in pivoting on the helicopter skid.

         2. Rappeller assumes an upright position facing inward toward the aircraft.

         3. Both rappeller and Safety NCO make final check of ropes, snaplinks, and rappel ring.

    (d) "DROP ROPES". The rappeller pushes the rope coiled on the log out of the aircraft with the guide hand.

    (e) "CHECK ROPES". The rappeller and the Safety NCO check the ropes, once dropped, to insure it is touching the ground and is not knotted or tangled.

    (f) "POSITION".

         1. The Safety NCO will motion the rappeller back to the "L" position.

         2. The rappeller assumes a "L" position on the helicopter skid and awaits the command to "GO".

    (g) "GO".

         1. The Safety NCO will designate rappellers to execute this command by vigorously pointing with extended arm and forefinger.

         2. The rappeller will flex his knees, straighten his legs vigorously, and loosen his brake hand

so as to drop 10 ft below the aircraft before again applying
his brake hand.

        3. Rappellers will apply their brake
hand at 10 to 15 ft intervals during descent to preclude ex-
cessive heating of the ropes.

        4. Upon reaching the ground, the rap-
peller will back out of his ropes and yell "OFF RAPPELL".

      (4) The sequence of exit from the UH-1D heli-
copter:

"LEFT FRONT and RIGHT REAR, followed by LEFT REAR
and RIGHT FRONT"

   3. CONCLUSIONS:

      a. Training time is approximately six (6) hours
per man if he has previous mountain rappelling training.
Approximately 24 hours are required if a man has no prior
experience.

      b. Current rappelling techniques allow a man to
rappel with bulky equipment such as radios, machineguns,
and rucksacks (using Chest Harness).

      c. The UH-1D helicopter can rappel up to six (6)
men simultaneously and up to eight (8) men in sequence.
The UH-1B can rappel four (4) men simultaneously and six
(6) men in sequence.

      d. Rappelling is a feasible and useful method of
air to ground delivery of personnel and equipment into combat jungle areas of operation where helicopter landing zones
may not be readily available.

      e. Helicopter rappelling qualification consists of:

      (1) Five (5) satisfactory tower exits (three (3)
with equipment).

      (2) Three (3) live helicopter rappels.

        (a) One without equipment.

        (b) Two (2) with equipment.

      f. A field expedient method of rappelling can be
employed by securing the rappel rope through at least three

(3) of the tie-down rings on the floor of the helicopter; coil rope with running end up; make helicopter rappel.

g. The points brought out in this chapter are designed as reference data for further instruction, and although extensive, are strictly key points. CAUTION: Guard against "OVERCONFIDENCE" at all stages of training. Remember: "COCKINESS BREEDS CARELESSNESS'

CHAPTER TWENTY-FOUR

STREAM CROSSING TECHNIQUES

1. GENERAL. The availability of ready-made bridges to a Ranger patrol is not only uncertain, but is highly doubtful. Therefore it is necessary to be able to negotiate expedient stream crossings. The patrol leader will need to know various techniques in order to make a successful stream crossing. The stream crossing team is designated and instructed to prepare ropes and equipment, and to conduct team rehearsals. This team should be highly proficient in the mechanics of a stream crossing. This proficiency is gained by realistic rehearsals, close inspections, organization, and good control.

2. ONE ROPE BRIDGE.
   a. Special Equipment Requirements:
      (1) Two snap links per piece of heavy equipment.
      (2) Two snap links per double butterfly knot.
      (3) One snap link per lifeguard bundle.
      (4) One snap link per person.
      (5) One utility rope per person.
      (6) One utility rope per piece of heavy equipment.
      (7) Sufficient length of 1/4" rope.
      (8) Sufficient length of 1/2" rope.
      (9) Laundry bags for holding clothes and equipment (optional).
   b. Plan for and organize the plan in stream crossing annex to the patrol order.
   c. Rehearsals and Inspections:
      (1) Rehearse the stream crossing team prior to the main rehearsal.
      (2) Rehearse the entire operation emphasizing

24.01

(a) Security and action on enemy contact.

(b) Actual establishment of the rope bridge.

(c) Individual preparations.

(d) Order of crossing.

(e) All signals and control measures.

(f) Reorganization.

(3) Conduct rehearsals as realistically as possible.

(4) Insure personnel are proficient in the mechanics of a stream crossing.

(5) Inspect for equipment completeness, correct rigging and preparation, and personnel knowledge and understanding of the operation.

d. Execution Phase:

(1) Steps for the establishment and conduct of a one-rope bridge stream crossing.

(a) Patrol leader halts short of the river, local security is established, and patrol leader conducts a recon of the area for the presence of the enemy and for crossing site suitability.

(b) Assistant patrol leader or security element leader, establishes security up and down stream while patrol leader briefs stream crossing team leader on anchor points.

(c) Stream crossing team commences to establish the rope bridge while patrol members begin individual preparations.

(d) Patrol leader supervises the entire operation, not just the establishment of the rope bridge. Leaders control and supervise subordinates.

(e) Noise and light discipline is enforced and security is alert.

(2) Stream crossing team erects the rope bridge as follows:

(a) Action of #1 man (near shore lifeguard)

24.02

<u>1</u>. Remove clothing.

<u>2</u>. Secure clothing, weapon and equipment in a single bundle using utility rope.

<u>3</u>. Bundle is placed in a secure position on the bank near the lifeguard's position.

<u>4</u>. He ties an end of the rope bow-line in a utility rope and places it on his arm. He ties an overhand knot in the running end for a life saving aid.

<u>5</u>. He puts on a B-7 life preserver.

<u>6</u>. He enters water.

<u>7</u>. No other patrol member enters the water prior to the near shore lifeguard.

(b) Actions of the #2 man (far shore lifeguard).

<u>1</u>. Removes clothing as was done by the near shore lifeguard.

<u>2</u>. Places bundle at the near shore anchor point.

<u>3</u>. He ties his utility rope around his waist using a round turn and a square knot with two half hitches.

(c) Actions of the #3 man (team leader).

<u>1</u>. He ties an end-of-the-rope bowline in the far shore end of the 1/4" tow rope leaving 9-12" loop.

<u>2</u>. He then joins the 1/4" and 1/2" manilla rope together with a double sheet bend leaving a foot of running end in the 1/4" rope.

<u>3</u>. He ties a B-7 life preserver in the juncture of the ropes using the running end of the 1/4" rope.

<u>4</u>. He ties an end-of-the-rope bowline in the near shore end of the 1/2" rope leaving 6-9" loop into which a snap link is inserted.

(d) When these actions have been completed, the following occurs:

24. 03

       1. The #2 man enters the water with the loop of the 1/4" rope attached to the utility rope around his waist by means of a snap link.

       2. The #2 man then moves up stream paralleling the bank to compensate for current, while the #3 man carefully feeds out the 1/4" rope.

       3. The #2 man swims to the far shore anchor point.

       4. The #2 man climbs the bank, moves to and behind the far shore anchor point.

       5. The #2 man pulls the remainder of the 1/4" rope and approximately 8-10 feet of the 1/2" rope across.

       6. The #2 man temporarily secures the ropes while the #3 man ties the double butterfly and completes the transport tightening system.

       7. The #2 man then takes up the slack in the rope and ties off the 1/2" rope at the far shore anchor point with a round-turn and two half-hitches with a quick release.

       8. The #3 man with the aid of two other men, tightens the rope and ties if off.

    e. Personnel then cross the rope and reorganize on the far shore.

    f. For further reference, refer to FM 21-50.

   3. PONCHO RAFT. Normally a poncho raft is constructed to cross rivers and streams when the current is not swift. A poncho raft is especially useful when the patrol is still dry and the patrol leader desires to keep the individual's equipment dry.

    a. Equipment Requirements:

      (1) Two ponchos.

      (2) Two rifles.

      (3) Two packs with individual equipment (fatigues, boots, socks, etc.).

b. Execution Phase. Steps for the construction of a poncho raft:

(1) Pair off the patrol/platoon in order to have the necessary equipment.

(2) Tie off the hood of one poncho and lay it out on the ground with the hood up.

(3) Weapons are then placed in the center of the poncho, butt to muzzle, approximately 18 inches apart.

(4) Next, packs and web gear are placed between the rifles with the two individuals placing their packs as far apart as possible.

(5) The two will then start undressing (bottom to top), first with their boots taking the laces completely out for subsequent use as tie downs.

(6) The boots are then placed forward of their packs (toward the center of the poncho) between the rifles.

(7) Next they remove their socks and use them to pad the front and rear sights of their rifles.

(8) They then continue to undress folding each item neatly and placing on top of their boots.

(9) Once all of the equipment is placed between the two weapons the poncho is snapped together. The snapped portion of the poncho is then held in the air and tightly rolled down at the center toward the equipment thus creating a pig tail at each end. The pig tailed ends are then folded in toward the center of the raft and tied off with a single bootlace.

(10) The other poncho is then layed out on the ground with the hood up and the first poncho with equipment is placed in its center. The second poncho is then snapped, rolled and tied in the same manner as the first poncho. The third and fourth bootlaces are then tied around the raft approximately one foot from each end for added security. The poncho raft is now complete.

24.05

4. FIELD EXPEDIENT EQUIPMENT. At times
while out on patrol you may be called upon to cross an
unfordable water obstacle without the proper equipment
for construction of a one rope bridge. Some of the equipment your patrol has can be used as a valuable asset.

   a. Equipment your patrol/platoon may be carrying which could be of use:

   (1) Commo wire.
   (2) Ammo cans.
   (3) Pistol belts.
   (4) Canteens.
   (5) Air mattresses.
   (6) Water proof bags.
   (7) Water cans.

   b. Execution Phase:

   (1) Commo wire can be pulled across the obstacle by a strong swimmer and tied off on a suitable
anchor point on the far shore with a round turn and two-
half hitches. The wire can then be pulled tight and tied off
in the same manner on the near shore. Care must be in-
sured not to pull the wire too tight as extreme tension will
cause it to fail under a load.

   (2) Ammo cans can be tied to the ends of a
pistol belt and used as water wings.

   (3) Five empty canteens tied to each end of a
pistol belt will support a non-swimmer.

   (4) Air mattresses will make excellent rafts.

   (5) Water proof bags, with an individual's
equipment placed inside, and the neck of the bag tied securely, will support a person.

   (6) An empty water can will float an individual
and his equipment safely across.

   (7) A pair of fatigue trousers tied off at each
of the ankles can be inflated and used as waterwings.

   c. Heavy equipment may be transported across
by constructing a litter with two poles and a poncho. The
litter is then supported by a poncho raft tied to each end.

CHAPTER TWENTY-FIVE

WATERBORNE OPERATIONS

1. GENERAL. Use of inland and coastal waterways may add flexibility, surprise, and speed to tactical operations. Use of these waterways will also increase the load carrying capacity of normally dismounted units.

2. EQUIPMENT.
   a. Reconnaissance Boat, Inflatable:
      Length: 3m
      Width: 1.3m
      Weight: 24 lbs; 33 lbs w/paddles and pump
      Crew: 1 coxswain, 2 paddlers
      Load: 500 lbs w/2-man crew, 300 lbs w/3-man crew.
   b. Plastic Assault Boat, M3:
      Length: 4.9m
      Width: 1.7m
      Weight: 300 lbs
      Crew: 1 coxswain, 10 paddlers
      Load: 3200 lbs or 15 men with equipment including crew
      Can be powered by 25HP outboard motor.
   c. Assault Boat, Pneumatic:
      Length: 5.2m
      Width: 1.8m
      Weight: 260 lbs
      Crew: 1 coxswain, 10 paddlers
      Load: 3300 lbs or 15 men with equipment including crew
      Can be powered by 25HP outboard motor.
   d. Landing Boat, Pneumatic:
      Length: 4m
      Width: 2m
      Weight: 150 lbs

Crew: 1 coxswain, 6 paddlers
Load: 10 men with equipment including crew.

3. ORGANIZATION.
   a. Assign each individual a specific boat position
   b. Designate a commander for each boat (normally coxswain).
   c. Designate navigator - observer team as necessary.
   d. Crew is positioned by following two systems.

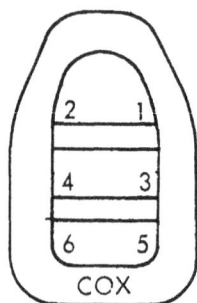

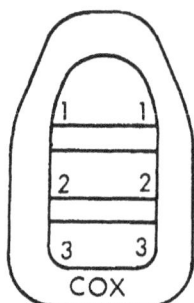

LONG COUNT
(passengers are num-
bered from front to
rear after crew is
numbered.)

SHORT COUNT
(Used for operation not
organization.)

   e. Crew Duties:
      (1) Coxswain:
         (a) Responsible for control of the boat
and action of the crew.

25.02

(b) Supervises the loading, lashing and distribution of equipment.

(c) Maintains the course and speed of the boat.

(2) Number 1 paddler is responsible for setting the stroke.

(3) Number 2 paddler is responsible for the stowage and use of the bowline.

(4) All paddlers are responsible for loading and lashing equipment in their respective compartment.

4. PREPARATION OF PERSONNEL AND EQUIPMENT.

a. All personnel will wear life preservers with quick release knot.

b. Harness will be worn unbuckled at the waist.

c. Rifle is worn diagonally across the back with a quick release on sling, muzzle pointed outboard.

d. Crew-served weapons, radios, ammunition and other bulk equipment must be lashed securely to the boat to prevent loss if boat should overturn.

e. Radios, batteries, and unboxed ammunition must be waterproofed.

f. Hot weapons must be cooled prior to being placed in the boat.

g. Pointed objects must be padded to prevent puncture of boat.

h. Equipment must be lashed only to the crosstubes or "snaplinked" to the life line around the floor in pneumatic boats. In pastic assault boat, equipment will be shored in place using wood or other suitable material and secured by running lines thru the carrying handles.

5. COMMANDS.

a. Short Count... Count off - Crew counts off their positions by pairs; i.e., 1, 2, 3, coxswain.

25.03

b. Long Count... Count off - Crew counts off their position by individual; i.e., 1, 2, 3, 4, 5, 6, coxswain.

c. Boat Stations - Crew takes positions along side of boat.

d. High Carry... Move (used for long distance moves overland):

(1) On the preparatory command of "high carry," the crew faces to the rear of the boat and squats down grasping carrying handles with the inboard hand.

(2) On the command "move," the crew swivels around, lifting the boat to their shoulders, so that the crew is standing and facing to the front with the boat on their inboard shoulders.

(3) Coxswain guides the crew during movement.

e. Low Carry... Move (used for short distance moves overland):

(1) On preparatory command of "low carry," the crew remains facing the front of the boat and grasps the carrying handles with the inboard hand.

(2) On the command "move," the crew stands up straight raising the boat approximately 6-8" off the ground.

(3) Coxswain guides the crew during movement.

f. Lower the Boat... Move: Crew lowers the boat gently to the ground using carrying handles.

g. Give Way Together - Crew paddles to front with Number 1 setting stroke.

h. Hold: Entire crew keeps paddles motionless in the water thereby stopping the boat.

i. Hold Left (Right): Left crew holds, right crew continues with previous command.

j. Back Paddle: Entire crew paddles backwards propelling the boat to the rear.

k. Back Paddle Left (Right): Left crew backpaddles causing boat to turn left, right crew continues with previous command.

25.04

l. Rest Paddles: Crew members place paddles on their laps with blades outboard. This command may be given to pairs; i.e., Number 1's rest paddles.

6. EMBARKING AND DEBARKING.
   a. When launching the crew maintains a firm grip on the boat until they are inside the boat; similarly, when beaching or debarking, they hold on to the boat until it is completely out of the water.
   b. Stay as low as possible when entering and leaving boat to avoid capsizing.
   c. The long count is a method of loading or unloading by which the boat crew embarks or debarks individually over the bow of the boat. It is used at river banks, on loading ramps and when deep water prohibits the use of other methods.
   d. The short count is a method of loading or unloading by which the boat crew embarks or debarks in pairs over the sides of the boat while the boat is in the water. It is used in shallow water and on ocean beaches with light surf.
   e. Beaching the boat is a method of debarking the entire crew at once into shallow water whereupon the boat is carried quickly out of the water.

7. RIVER MOVEMENT.
   a. Characteristics of Rivers:
      (1) Know local conditions prior to embarking on river movement.
      (2) A curve is a turn in the river course.
      (3) A reach is a straight portion of river between two curves.
      (4) A slough is a dead end branch from a river. They are normally quite deep and can be distinguished from the true river by their lack of current.

25.05

(5) The current in a narrow part of a reach is normally greater than in a wide portion.

(6) The current is greatest on the outside of a curve, the sandbars and shallow water are found on the inside of the curve.

(7) Sandbars are located at those points where a tributary feeds into the main body of a river or stream.

(8) The coxswain must watch the water for obstacles and overhanging vegetation and projections from the bank.

b. Navigation: The unit commander is responsible for navigation. There are three acceptable methods of river navigation which he may use:

(1) Checkpoint and general route: This method is used when the drop site is marked by a well-defined checkpoint and the waterway is not confused by many branches and tributaries. It is best used during daylight hours and for short distances.

(2) Navigator-observer method: This is the most accurate means of river navigation and can be used effectively in all light conditions.

(a) Equipment needed:
Compass
Photo map (1st choice)
Topo map (2d choice)
Poncho (for night use)
Pencil
Flashlight (for night use).

(b) Navigator is positioned in center of boat and does not paddle. During hours of darkness, he uses his flashlight under the poncho to check his map.

(c) Navigator places his compass in a fixed position oriented with the long axis of the boat thereby keeping a constant check on the boat's heading. He compares this heading with the azimuth of each reach which he determines from his map and charts the boat's location on his map.

25.06

(d) The observer keeps the navigator informed of configuration of the river by announcing curves, sloughs and stream junctions.

(e) The navigator compares this information with his map and informs the observer of curves, sloughs, reaches and stream junctions from the map and when these are confirmed the navigator confirms the boat's location on his map.

(f) The observer keeps the navigator informed of turns due to crew failure to avoid confusing the navigator. The observer may also take the azimuth of reaches to confirm the navigator's heading and map azimuth.

(g) A strip map drawn on clear acetate backed with luminous tape may be used. The drawing may be to scale or a schematic. It should show all curves and the azimuth and distance of all reaches. It may also show terrain features, stream junctions and sloughs.

(3) Time distance method: This is the least desirable method due to variations in paddling speed and river velocity. It is difficult to establish an exact travel time for river movement and this method should be used in conjunction with one of the other methods.

8. SURF OPERATIONS.

   a. Launching:

      (1) Use short count method of loading.

      (2) Crew must keep their weight well forward until beyond the surf.

      (3) The bow of the boat must be kept perpendicular to the waves.

   b. Landing:

      (1) The stern of the boat must be kept perpendicular to the waves.

      (2) Crew must keep their weight well to the rear after entering surf.

      (3) Paddlers do not look seaward.

25.07

(4) Crew debarks using the short count or beaching method.

(5) Crew holds onto the boat until it is out of the water.

9. FORMATIONS. Various boat formations can be used both day and night for control, speed and security. The choice of which is used depends on the tactical situation and the discretion of the patrol leader. Those most commonly used are:

a. Inverted Vee.

b. Line.

c. File.

10. SECURING THE LANDING SITE. The landing site must be secured before the waterborne force lands. One method of securing the landing site is for one boat to land, recon the landing area, secure the landing site and then signal the remaining boats to land.

CHAPTER TWENTY-SIX

HANDLING OF KIA'S

1. GENERAL: Although the Graves Registration Section of the Quartermaster Corps provides identification, registration and burial, the patrol leader may be faced with a situation where he is forced to bury personnel. Emergency burials will be carried out so as to conform with accepted principles of hygiene, to obtain the maximum of safety from marauding animals and looting, and to provide maximum chance of subsequent recovery by friendly forces.

a. Burial Procedure: With the exception of United States personnel, all personal effects, including all personal and official papers (assure that no intelligence documents are left) will be removed from the remains and placed in a suitable receptacle. One identification tag/disk must be buried with the corpse. The second will be placed in a receptacle with the personal effects. In the case of United States personnel, all personal effects and one identification tag will be buried with the remains and the second carried back to your unit.

b. The following is a checklist for the patrol leader to follow:

(1) The minimum depth of the grave should be 3 feet (0.90 m), deeper if possible.

(2) Remove one identification tag and any intelligence information. Leave the second tag with the body.

(3) It is recommended that the body be wrapped in a shelter half, poncho, blanket, etc, whenever possible.

(4) Whenever practicable, a brief burial service of the appropriate religion should be held, or in any event, a prayer said.

(5) Eight-digit coordinates should be recorded to assure recovery of the body. Burial near a natural terrain feature aids in the location of the grave.

(6) Report the location, by coordinates, describing the terrain feature to the unit commander and unit chaplain. Give other information such as: name, rank, serial number, circumstances, etc. Also, give identification tags to the unit commander.

2. For further reference, refer to FM 10-63 and AR 638-30.

CHAPTER TWENTY SEVEN

COUNTERGUERRILLA OPERATIONS

CONTENTS:

PART I - SMALL UNIT COUNTERGUERRILLA TACTICS AND TECHNIQUES

1. GUERRILLA TACTICS AND TECHNIQUES: Prior to discussing counterguerrilla warfare, the basic characteristics of guerrilla warfare must be understood.

    a. The basic prerequisites for successful guerrilla operations are:

        (1) Assistance and support from the local indigenous population of the area of operations.

           (a) This assistance may be voluntary or forced.

           (b) Assistance generally includes, intelligence information, food, clothing, recovery areas, transportation and medical support.

        (2) Aid that may be received from an outside sponsoring power.

           (a) Supplies and training.

           (b) Leadership, funds, moral and psychological support.

        (3) Vast knowledge of the terrain in which the guerrillas must operate.

        (4) Intelligent leadership.

        (5) Strong, centralized control of the overall guerrilla effort.

        (6) Strict discipline.

        (7) Maintenance of extensive intelligence and logistic nets.

        (8) A will to fight and motivation.

    b. After the guerrilla leader has established his force, he emphasizes the following characteristics of guerrilla warfare in his operations against the enemy:

        (1) <u>Surprise</u>: The guerrilla gains surprise by striking where the enemy is weak and when he leasts expects an attack. He selects his time and place of attack, based on reliable intelligence and sound security.

        (2) <u>Mobility</u>: Guerrillas stress rapid individual and small unit cross country foot mobility.

(3) Dispersion of forces: Guerrillas generally conduct small scale operations and attempt to disperse among the civilian population when pursued too closely, or hard pressed.

    c. Considering the prerequisites outlined in 1 above, and emphasizing the characteristics outlined in 2 above, the guerrilla force conducts the following basic offensive operations against the enemy:

(1) Harassment operations to include terrorism assassination, and psychological warfare.

(2) Ambushes.

(3) Raids.

2. SMALL UNIT COUNTERGUERRILLA TACTICS AND TECHNIQUES:

    a. Mission: The mission of the counterguerrilla force is simple -- it is to kill guerrillas. The guerrilla is always the objective - not key terrain or installations. To accomplish their mission requires the location, isolation and final destruction, or capture of the guerrillas. The three phases of counterguerrilla action are at times conducted in three separate phases, but most often the transition from one phase to the next is rapid and automatic. And often the isolation and distruction phases are conducted concurrently as will be apparent in the discussion of the basic counterguerrilla warfare tactics and techniques to follow.

    b. Definition:

(1) Location of the guerrilla: To pinpoint the location of the guerrilla, either moving or halted, through use of ground patrols, static observation posts or surveillance sites, aerial observation, aerial photography, or through intelligence information provided by numerous other sources.

(2) Isolation of the guerrilla: To seal off all escape routes and concurrently prevent reinforcement or assistance from indigenous or outside resources.

27.03

(3) Destruction of the guerrilla: To kill or capture the isolated guerrillas using fire and maneuver.

c. The best guerrilla fighter or counterguerrilla
soldier is one who is first, well versed in small unit tactics
and techniques and second, one who has a thorough knowledge of guerrilla operations and is capable of using the guerrilla tactics of harassment, ambush, and surprise raid
against the guerrilla.

d. In addition to those tactics or type operations
indicated in 3 above, the following basic type operation or
tactics and techniques are utilized extensively by the small
unit counterguerrilla force:

(1) Encirclement and Hammer and Anvil: Once
a stationary or fixed guerrilla force, or fixed installation,
is located, the counterguerrilla force normally attempts to
encircle it, thus isolating the objective. The encirclement
is normally the initial step of the isolation and destruction
phases of any counterguerrilla operation. This technique
can be applied even in the pursuit of a guerrilla force by en-
velopment of the withdrawing guerrillas by the counterguerrilla force, thus stopping them at which time the encirclement can then be completed.

*Figure 1 - Initial Encirclement

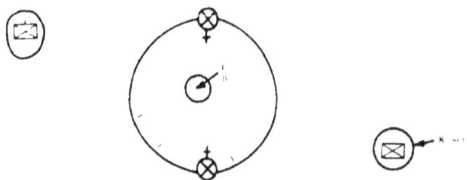

*Initial Encirclement
Phase Line Blue

Encirclement operations are best carried out by battalion
size and larger units; however, a company size force can
conduct successful encirclement operations against small
guerrilla elements. There are certain factors affecting the
ability of the company in conduct of an encirclement. These
are:

(a) Mobility means available.

(b) Type terrain and concealment afforded
within the area.

(c) The degree of surprise obtained.

(d) The speed with which the encirclement
is accomplished.

(e) The supporting fires available.

(f) The determination and state of training
of the counterguerrilla force.

After the guerrillas have been isolated by the encirclement,
the counterguerrilla force completes the destruction using
the "hammer and anvil" technique.

Figure 2.   Hammer and Anvil from the Encirclement

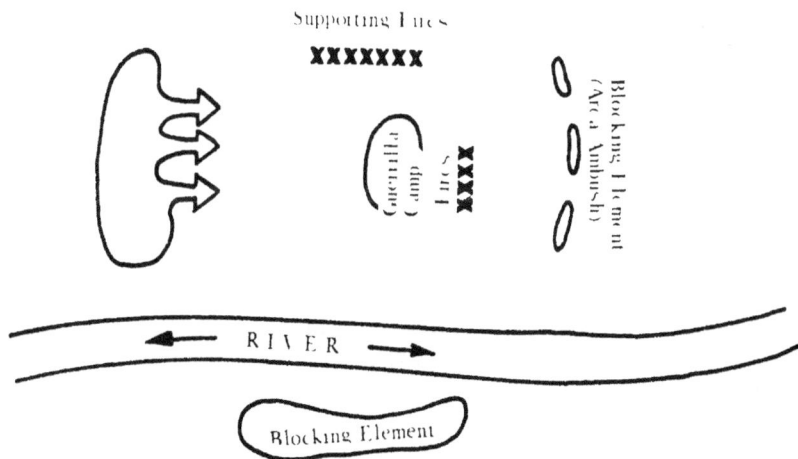

27.05

The hammer, or attacking element, attacks from the initial
line of encirclement, killing or capturing the guerrillas or
driving them into the anvil, or the blocking or area ambush
forces. The attacking element stops at a predesignated limit of advance. The blocking or area ambush force then completes the destruction of those guerrillas attempting to escape. Supporting artillery and aerial fires are employed as
appropriate and as available. The operation depicted in
Figure 2 can be conducted by a company size unit.

       (2) Another variation of the hammer and anvil
technique can be conducted from the pursuit.

Figure 3 - Hammer and Anvil from Pursuit

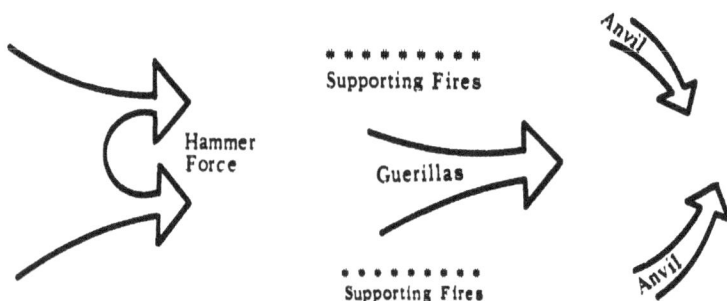

The pursuing, or hammer, force maintains contact and direct pressure on the fleeing guerrillas. Supporting artillery and aerial fires are employed on the guerrillas, and on
the flanks of the axis of pursuit. A blocking or anvil force
is then placed in position using helicopters or other means
of rapid transportation. The direct pressure force stops at
a designated limit of advance and the anvil force with all
available supporting fires completes the destruction of the
guerrillas.

(3) Search and destroy: A technique utilized extensively in counterguerrilla warfare is the search and destroy operation. The counterguerrilla force, employing various techniques of area search, attempts to locate and make contact with the guerrillas. Once contact is made, the search force is then reorganized and then becomes the destruction force using maximum available supporting artillery and aerial fires. If the guerrilla force is superior in strength or firepower, the force making the initial contact attempts to maintain contact until reserves or reaction forces can be committed to complete the destruction of the guerrilla force. Maintenance of contact is a very important aspect of this type operation. The following are three basic search techniques which can be used effectively by a platoon size search and destroy force.

Figure 4 - Fan Patrolling Method

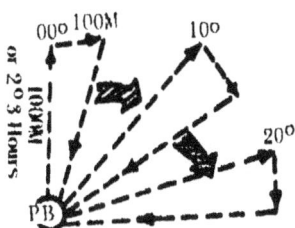

The platoon established a patrol base in or in the vicinity of its assigned zone. From this patrol base, subordinate patrols are dispatched and search along predesignated azimuths for a specified distance or period of time, at the end of the 1st leg, patrols make a 90 degree turn to the right, move for 100 meters, then turn again and return to the patrol base on a predesignated azimuth. The same procedure is repeated until the entire area has been searched.

27.07

Figure 5 - River or Stream Search Method

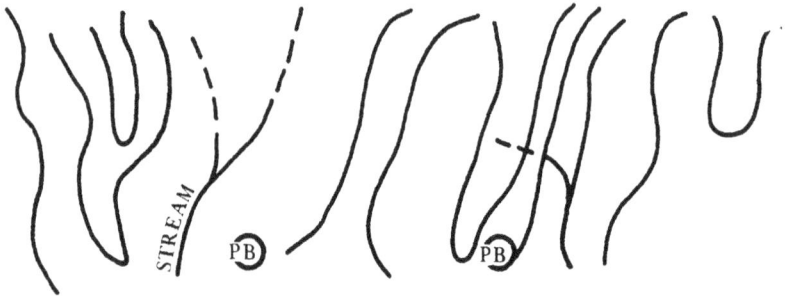

Guerrillas locate their bases near a source of water. Locate the main streams in an area, establish a patrol base,
and beginning on one end of side of assigned zone, preferably the downstream end, search along the main streams and
tributaries observing the water for debris or other evidence
of human presence upstream. Search along one side of a
stream then back along the other side, or using two patrols
abreast, search both sides simultaneously.

Figure 6 - Cross Grain Search Method

27.08

Most trails in a given area will generally follow the contours of the terrain. Begin the search at a known point and move on a predesignated azimuth across the terrain or across corridors. If a clear trail or indication of human movement off a beaten path is discovered, determine the direction of movement and follow the trail, eventually catching up to the personnel making the trail. Search along, or parallel to, these trails in both directions. It is important that location on the ground and on the map is known at all times. Once contact has been made with the guerrillas using the search methods described, then the search phase of the search and destroy mission is completed and the destruction beings.

(4) <u>Reinforcement or reaction operations:</u>

(a) Another type operation a counterguerrilla force may conduct is reinforcement of a friendly fixed critical installation in event it is seriously threatened by guerrillas. Plans for execution of this type operation are called contingency plans. When preparing such plans, the counterguerrilla force commander effects detailed coordination with the friendly security force at the installation, reconnoiters the assigned area of responsibility, prepares and rehearses these reinforcement, or relief plans and is prepared to execute the plan or order at any time from any location within the area of operation.

(b) The objective of operations of this type is twofold:

<u>1.</u> To relieve, or provide assistance to, the friendly security force under attack and to prevent destruction or seizure of the installation by the guerrillas.

<u>2.</u> To kill or capture as many guerrillas as possible in the process of reinforcement.

27.09

Figure 7- Contingency Plan for Reaction or Reinforcement

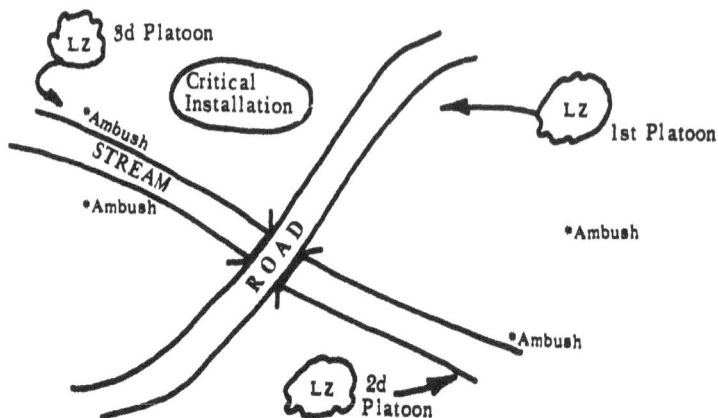

Figure 7 depicts a company utilizing three platoons for reinforcement of a critical installation. One platoon lands by
helicopter at a prescribed landing zone conducts direct reinforcement of the installation over a designated route. The
other two platoons land by helicopter in separate LZ's and
move to and establish ambushes along likely guerrilla withdrawal routes.

    (5) Pursuit:
        (a) When contact is made with a guerrilla
force, the most likely reaction will be to inflict maximum
casualties on the counterguerrilla force and then break contact and withdraw or disperse. The counterguerrilla force
must therefore be particularly adept in the conduct of pursuit operations. A pursuit is the maintenance with, and the
continuation of offensive action against the withdrawing guer
rilla force. The pursuit can be conducted by any size force

and the pursuit force usually is organized into two elements
--the direct pressure force and the encircling force(s). Rap
id assistance must normally be provided the unit making con·
tact with the guerrillas so that it can maintain pressure
against the fleeing force, stop it, or envelop it, and complete destruction of the force.

Figure 8 - Conduct of Pursuit

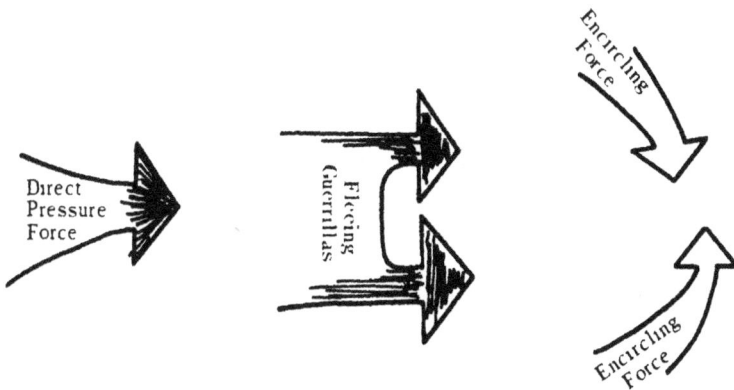

The direct pressure force pursues and maintains contact
with, and pressure against, the fleeing guerrillas. The encircling force(s), conducts local envelopments to stop the
guerrillas or cut them off, and destroy them.
　　　　　(b) A most important aspect of the pursuit
is that the direct pressure element must maintain constant
contact with the guerrillas.
　　　　(6) Road Clearance Operations:
　　　　　　　(a) Road clearance constitutes the clearance
of guerrilla mines and demolitions from a specified section
of road, highway or railroad, and the clearance of both
sides of the road in question, of guerrillas and the threat of

27.11

ambush. The actual clearance of any route should take place as late as possible prior to movement of convoys or foot columns.

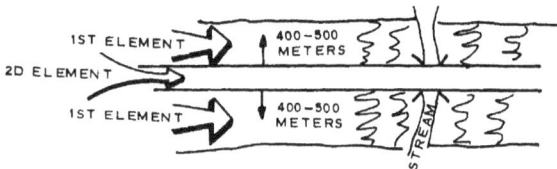

Figure 9. Road Clearance

1st Element Forward – Searches for command mine leads and personnel

One element physically clears the roadway be removing or destroying mines, boobytraps and obstacles. The second element clears an area on both sides of the road out to max· imum effective small arms range from the road (400-500 meters). This is accomplished by physically sweeping the area with foot troops on both sides of the road. (Fig 9)

   (b) Artillery and aerial fire support are utilized to the maximum against likely ambush sites and in a reconnaissance by fire role prior to the conduct of sweeps by foot troops. Small ambush forces may be dropped off and remain concealed in the vicinity of the most likely ambush sites until the planned movement on the road has been completed.

3. FIRE SUPPORT: In addition to the uses of artillery and aerial fires already mentioned in paragraph 4 above, these fires can also be utilized very effectively as follows:

a. To provide all around security during movement and at halts.

b. To canalize enemy movement.

c. In the defense of static positions or installations.

d. Reconnaissance by fire.

e. To seal off avenues of impress and egress of guerrilla forces.

f. To deliver harassing fires on suspect guerrilla locations or routes.

g. To deny certain areas, and routes of approach and withdrawal to the guerrillas.

h. To provide preparatory or suppressive fires in support of airmobile and other offensive operations against guerrillas.

i. To fire on own positions, installations, outposts, or strongpoints, in event guerrillas overrun these positions.

4. FORWARD AIR CONTROLLER (FAC) PROCEDURES:

a. Forward air controllers are trained air force personnel who work with ground units in directing aircraft in close air support. If for some reason these personnel are not available, the ground unit leader must be capable of assisting or guiding tactical aircraft pilots onto enemy targets. The procedures used by the personnel of the supported ground unit for this purpose are called forward air controller (FAC) procedures.

b. In order for the small unit leader to properly guide close air support aircraft pilots, there are three things he must be able to do. These are:

(1) Identify himself, and establish and maintain communications with the pilot or flight leader.

(2) Mark or identify friendly unit location(s).

(3) Give location and description of target.

c. Identification and establishment of communications is normally by voice radio using the SOI that is currently in effect.

d. Friendly positions can be marked by several methods. Some are:

(1) VS-17 Air panels.

(2) Signal mirrors.

(3) Smoke grenades.

(4) Terrain association.

(5) Lights or flares.

(6) Clock system in conjunction with aircraft tract.

e. Targets can be marked in any of the following ways:

(1) Azimuth and distance from a reference point.

(2) Terrain association.

(3) Clock system in conjunction with aircraft tract.

(4) Marking enemy locations by fire or smoke.

f. Radio transmissions should be short, clear, accurate and to the point.

PART II - COMBAT INTELLIGENCE

1. INTELLIGENCE COLLECTION AND PROCESSING PROCEDURES:

a. Terms and Definitions:

(1) Combat Intelligence: . . . "That knowledge of the enemy, weather, and terrain, required by a commander in the planning and conduct of tactical operations." In counterguerrilla operations, knowledge of the local indigenous population is also essential.

(2) EEI: Essential elements of information . . . "are critical items of information regarding enemy, weather

27.14

and terrain required by a commander at a particular time to relate with other information and intelligence to assist in reaching a logical conclusion." There are usually broad, general questions used at brigade level and higher commands such as: Where are the guerrillas located?

(3) Request for information: This is a term used to describe more specific questions, extracted from EEI at battalion, company, platoon and patrol levels, which are applicable to the respective unit mission, area of operation and capability. Such requests are normally issued as part of the operation order, and give focus to the unit's intelligence gathering effort. Each commander adds a few additional questions or requests the answer to which will assist in accomplishment of the specific mission.

b. Processing information into intelligence: This is a simple mental process using common sense.

(1) Observe: (Keep code word salute in mind while observing.)

(2) Record information: (Use code word salute as format.)

S - Size - 8-man guerrilla patrol.

A - Activity - moving west on trial, man packing supplies.

L - Location - at EJ178834. ·

U - Unit - unknown.

T - Time - at 1030 22 April 1966.

E - Equipment - 5 armed with carbines and 3 armed with 22 caliber pistols.

(3) Evaluate: (is the source of information reliable? Is it first hand or second hand information?)

(4) Analyze: (Compare with other information - are there reports from other sources of the same enemy patrol?)

(5) Conclusion: (Formulate a conclusion based on your analysis) (The guerrillas may be transporting supplies to a cache site)

and terrain required by a commander at a particular time to relate with other information and intelligence to assist in reaching a logical conclusion." There are usually broad, general questions used at brigade level and higher commands such as: Where are the guerrillas located?

(3) Request for information: This is a term used to describe more specific questions, extracted from EEI at battalion, company, platoon and patrol levels, which are applicable to the respective unit mission, area of operation and capability. Such requests are normally issued as part of the operation order, and give focus to the unit's intelligence gathering effort. Each commander adds a few additional questions or requests the answer to which will assist in accomplishment of the specific mission.

b. Processing information into intelligence: This is a simple mental process using common sense.

(1) Observe: (Keep code word salute in mind while observing.)

(2) Record information: (Use code word salute as format.)

S - Size - 8-man guerrilla patrol.

A - Activity - moving west on trial, man packing supplies.

L - Location - at EJ178834.

U - Unit - unknown.

T - Time - at 1030 22 April 1966.

E - Equipment - 5 armed with carbines and 3 armed with 22 caliber pistols.

(3) Evaluate: (is the source of information reliable? Is it first hand or second hand information?)

(4) Analyze: (Compare with other information - are there reports from other sources of the same enemy patrol?)

(5) Conclusion: (Formulate a conclusion based on your analysis) (The guerrillas may be transporting supplies to a cache site)

27.15

c. Handling of prisoners of war:
   (1) Disarm.
   (2) Search for documents and arms, the searcher should never place himself between the guard and the prisoner.
   (3) Silence - tie, blindfold, gag, and tag.

Sample Prisoner Tag:

NAME: Wun Hung Lo

DATE & TIME OF CAPTURE: 241300 Jan 66

LOCATION AND CIRCUMSTANCES: EJ124832
                              Hiding in Bldg

CAPTURING UNIT: "H" Co. , 75th Inf. (Ranger) (Abn)

(If names are unknown, number the prisoners in sequence of capture. Use the same number to identify documents and other items taken from the prisoner.)
   (4) Separate - leaders, guerrillas, foreign advisors, civilians, (and females from males).
   (5) Safeguard - maintain adequate guard or security at all times.
   (6) Speed - after battlefield interrogation, evacuate to higher headquarters as soon as possible.
d. Organization for area or installation intelligence search: To be properly prepared for intelligence search, the following additional duties are recommended for each squad:

Duty	No Personnel	Special Equipment
2 search teams	4	
2 POW/Search teams	4	Blindfolds, ropes, tags, gags
2 interrogators	2	
1 recorder	1	Message book
1 interpreter (if available)	1	
	12 personnel	

27. 16

e. A recommended procedure for search of a guer-rilla base or village.

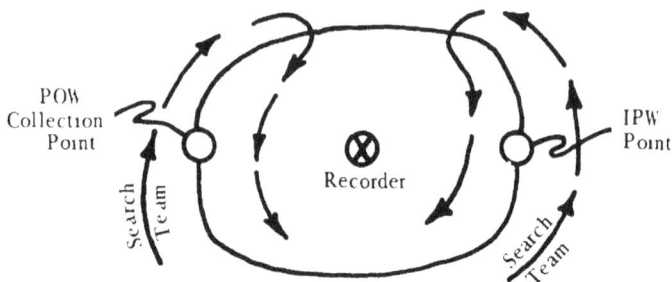

(1) Insure that the area is secured by the other squads of the platoon.
(2) Divide the base in half and designate POW collection and IPW points.
(3) Insure that IPW point is out of sight and hearing of the POW collection point.
(4) Search outside as well as inside the area or installation occupied by the guerrilla force.
(5) Interrogators and interpreters occupy desig-nated positions.
(6) Report information collected to the recorder
(7) The squad leader supervises the overall ac-tivities of the squad.

2. BATTLEFIELD INTERROGATION:
    a. General:
        (1) Interrogation is a means of obtaining useful, timely information through questioning.
        (2) Battlefield interrogation is normally brief and pertinent to the local tactical situation.

27.17

(3) The basic steps in interrogation are:

(a) <u>Planning</u> - Determine the objectives of interrogation based upon the immediate tactical knowledge needed and from the current requests for information then prepare a general line of questioning.

(b) <u>Approach</u> - Decide which approach can best be applied to the subject. (See 2b)

(c) <u>Questioning</u> - Use basic interrogatives (who, what, when, where, why and how). Avoid leading questions. Observe subjects' reactions and maintain control of conversation.

(d) <u>Recording</u> - If possible, avoid taking notes in view of the subject.

(e) <u>Dissemination</u> - Report results of the interrogation through chain of command.

b. <u>Basic Questioning Techniques:</u>

(1) <u>Direct approach:</u> No attempt is made to conceal the purpose of the interrogation. Give the subject an opportunity to talk. This is the most common approach due to the normal lack of time.

(2) <u>Rapid-fire questioning:</u> This technique is designed to keep the subject off balance and on the defensive with rapid questions. It is best employed using two interrogators.

(3) <u>Futility:</u> This technique attempts to convince the subject his cause is hopeless and that it is useless to withhold information.

(4) <u>Hot and cold:</u> A technique applied to a subject of little intelligence. The first interrogator is harsh to the subject, then second interrogator intervenes and treats subject kindly in an attempt to gain his confidence.

(5) <u>Self-induced fear:</u> This technique points out the uncertainty of the subject's fate (as with a wounded prisoner), and frightens the subject into talking.

(6) <u>Deception:</u> Initially questions are asked, the answers to which are known by the interrogator to cause the subject to believe that the interrogator knows all the answers, and that it is useless to withhold information.

c. Special Questioning Techniques:
  (1) Map tracking techniques: Lead the subject through a discussion with the aid of a map, this will aid in control and will insure greater validity of information.
  (2) Show photos of guerrilla leaders, or other wanted persons, to subjects and observe facial expressions.
  (3) Use of interpreters:
    (a) If possible, avoid using interpreters due to the disadvantages of: misunderstanding, difficulty in establishing rapport, inability to use certain interrogation techniques, and the security risks involved.
    (b) Brief the interpreter to absolutely avoid side conversations with the POW and instruct him to translate questions and answers exactly as stated.
    (c) Position the interpreter to the side or rear away from the POW's line of vision. The POW should always be facing the interpreter.

3. TRACKING: The ability to track and interpret trail signs is particularly valuable in counterguerrilla warfare. The basic concepts of tracking are:
  a. Displacement:
    (1) Footprints.
    (a) The last person in a party normally leaves a clear set of footprints, study these for distinguishing marks (sole and heel design, imprint and size). Size should be measured and this measurement retained for future use.
    (b) Deep toe marks in normally spaced prints indicate the person was carrying a heavy load.
    (c) Deep toe marks in widely spaced prints indicate the person was running.
    (d) Water in foot prints made in low, marshy areas will remain muddied for approximately 1 hour.

27.19

(2) Foliage.
(a) Displaced grass and vines will be pointing in direction of movement.
(b) Rocks and leaves overturned will display darker under sides.
(c) Scuffed bark and foliage will display a lighter color.

b. Staining:
(1) Blood stains. Fresh red blood stains turn to brown after a short period of time. Observe for stains on leaves and underbrush and note their height. This may indicate the location of the wound.
(2) Mud. Mud carried from one area to another may provide an indication of where party came from. Water is always muddied downstream from fording sites.

c. Littering: Capitalize on the poor discipline of littering guerrillas. Observe for scraps of paper and cloth and abandoned equipment marking trails.

d. Weathering:
(1) Rain tends to round out or obliterate footprints depending on intensity of rain. Rain will flatten paper and cloth litter.
(2) Sunlight will cause crumbling of the moist dirt ridge normally outlining a fresh footprint within 1 hour. Light colored litter becomes yellowed from sunlight in 2-3 days. Observe for the difference in color between the sides facing the ground and the side facing the sun, to determine the age of litter.
(3) Wind displaces leaves, twigs and small debris into footprints. Prints should be examined to determine whether the debris was crushed by the party being tracked, or was blown into the tracks by the wind.
(4) Weather elements will cause some exposed metal to rust. Spots of rust will normally appear on rims of opened cans within 12 hours. This caries with specific geographic locations.

27.20

e. Interpretation: Analyze all the factors of displacement, littering, staining and weathering to determine the who, what, where, when, how, and why of the tracked party, from the various trail signs.

f. General Rules Utilized in Tracking:

(1) If possible, observe tracks by looking toward sun.

(2) If tracks are lost, mark the last trail sign and search for the trail in concentric circles from the marked point.

(3) Remember the date of the last rain and significant wind to determine the age of trail signs.

(4) Become familiar with weathering effects peculiar to the specific area of operations.

4. COUNTERINTELLIGENCE: Counterintelligence measures normally employed by the small counterguerrilla unit are merely those of stealth, camouflage, deception and security to enhance attainment of surprise and to counter guerrilla surprise and intelligence efforts.

a. Camouflage:

(1) Individual camouflage. Tone down the exposed skin surfaces and break the outline of the body and equipment. Sand bags, camouflage sticks, vegetation, salvage camouflage nets, and general purpose nets that conform with light conditions and surrounding vegetation may be used for camouflage.

(2) Position camouflage.

(a) Select positions with the lowest possible silhouette.

(b) Move under rather than through bushes.

(c) Avoid exposure of the undersides of the vegetation used for camouflage.

(d) If possible, camouflage completely to prevent detection from all sides (spider holes or human trees).

(3) Trail concealment.

(a) If possible, avoid areas and locations which leave clearly defined trail signs such as open sandy areas and muddy locations.

(b) Instruct the rear most personnel in the formation to erase all footprints and sign of movement with branches and to pick up or camouflage discarded litter.

b. Deception:

(1) Enter and depart patrol base at a 90 degree angle to previous or intended azimuth of movement.

(2) Cross roads and open areas at an abrupt angle to the true movement azimuth and continue for a short distance beyond. If possible, cross these areas in multiple angles to confuse and deceive the guerrilla.

(3) Never eat and sleep in the same location for more than 24 hours.

c. Security Measures:

(1) Restrict digging, chopping and other noise making activities to predetermined times of high noise background. This is normally during daylight hours.

(2) Light and noise discipline should be strictly enforced, cooking firewood should be dry and as smokeless as possible.

(3) Bury and camouflage all refuse.

(4) Functional early warning systems should always be employed, communication wire or vines attached to each person, and cans with pebbles to rattle when disturbed are useful methods.

5. THE USE OF SMELL, TOUCH AND HEARING IN OBTAINING COMBAT INTELLIGENCE: Particularly in night combat situations, the ability to use these three human senses to obtain information is necessary and important.

a. Odors detected at a distance from a village or camp can be useful in determining guerrilla activity.

27.22

(1) The smell of cigarette smoke can be detected up to 1/4 mile from source under certain wind conditions.

(2) The smell of fish, garlic and other foods being cooked can be detected for a considerable distance.

(3) The odor of bath soap, insect repellents, and lotions can be detected for a considerable distance.

(4) Explosives, certain soils and burning wood emit distinctive odors.

b. The sense of touch must be used while searching tunnels, buildings and dead guerrillas at night.

(1) To determine the identify of an object by touch, feel for shape, moisture, temperature and texture of the object.

(2) Use branches or a fine piece of vine attached to an expended cartridge to detect tripwires.

(3) The temperature of objects may indicate when last used.

(4) Jagged edges may indicate recent destruction of items.

(5) Moisture normally remains around the belt and boot tops of persons approximately 2 hours after they have been submerged in water.

c. Hearing: The guerrilla makes sounds which will often aid you in determining his location and activity. Counterguerrilla force members should become familiar with the following sounds peculiar to their area of operations:

(1) Sounds of human laughing, talking, walking, running, and crawling.

(2) Sounds of weapons loading, bolt movement and firing. Particularly important is the ability to differentiate between the sounds of weapons normally used by the guerrilla and those of the counterguerrilla force. (Example M-16 vs Carbine)

27.23

(3) Duller noises are usually associated with larger caliber weapons and sharper noises with smaller caliber high velocity weapons when fired.

(4) Animal and bird distress calls indicating presence of personnel should be recognized.

(5) In addition, the importance of the ability to use the "flash-bang" and "cracks-thump" techniques to determine range to weapons firing, or explosions, is readily apparent.

6. AREA SURVEILLANCE OPERATIONS:

a. Definition: Area surveillance is a method of gaining information of enemy activity by the placement of static surveillance, or observation teams throughout a defined area to observe and report information.

b. General:

(1) Characteristics of surveillance operations:

(a) Purpose: To gain information.

(b) Secrecy is necessary to prevent compromise.

(c) Physical contact with the enemy should be avoided if possible.

(d) Surveillance is conducted from stationary concealed positions which offer good observation.

(e) Patience is necessary.

(f) The intelligence information gained is the basis for offensive actions.

(2) The primary reasons for initiation of surveillance operations are:

(a) Incomplete intelligence reports.

(b) Lack of enemy information.

(c) For confirmation or verification of specific information, or EEI obtained from other sources.

(d) As a preparation for offensive action.

c. Planning:
(1) Concepts. The unit commander can assign the following to subordinate elements:
(a) Specific surveillance points.
(b) Sectors of responsibility.
(c) A combination of the above.
(2) Surveillance points.
(a) Are concealed to prevent detection.
(b) Provide maximum observation of roads, trails, open areas and all natural lines of draft.
(c) Are sited to enhance communications.
(3) Organization and Equipment (example).
(a) 2-3 surveillance team per squad.
(b) Surveillance team (3 or 4 men).

	Duty	Specific Equipment
1	Team Leader	Binocular
2	Recorder	Message book, map
3	RTO	PRC-4/9 or PRC-10
4	Security	

d. Conduct of Surveillance:
(1) Infiltrate or move into positions at night.
(2) Inactivity - 1 resting, 2 awake, all awake during activity.
(3) Maintain 360 degree security.
(4) Record - report - interpret.
(5) Perform debriefing and dissemination at each echelon.
(6) Keep situation map and messages.
(7) Analysis by each echelon for possible offensive action based on intelligence obtained.
e. Interpretation of Information: Determine from observation:
(1) Best ambush locations.
(2) Distance, time and pattern of guerrilla movement.

27.25

(3) Possible location of guerrilla caches, bases recovery or rest areas, etc.

(4) Reasons guerrilla activity observed.

f. Intelligence Briefing: Upon arrival in an area of operations an intelligence briefing should be conducted for the counterguerrilla force. The briefing should include the following items:

(1) Weather.

(2) Prominent terrain features and characteristics, to include military aspects of terrain (observation and fields of fire, cover and concealment, foot movement experience factors, critical points, and critical terrain).

(3) Characteristics of the local population.

(4) Guerrilla factors:

(a) Objectives.

(b) Order of battle.

(c) Past activities.

(d) Capabilities and techniques, to include indicators of future activity.

g. Unit combat intelligence policy and procedures.

CHAPTER TWENTY-EIGHT

PRAYERS

The Twenty-Third Psalm (for all faiths)

"The Lord is my shepherd, I shall not want;
He maketh me to lie down in green pastures.
He leadeth me beside the still waters;
He restoreth my soul.
He leadeth me in the paths of righteousness for his name's
    sake.
Yea though I walk through the valley of the shadow of death
I fear no evil;
For Thou art with me;
Thy rod and Thy staff,
They comfort me.
Thou preparest a table before me in the pressence of mine
    enemies;
Thou anointest my head with oil;
My cup runneth over.
Surely goodness and mercy shall follow me all the days of
    my life;
And I shall dwell in the house of the Lord forever."

Protestant Prayer

"O God, my Father, I come to Thee through trust in Thy
Son, the Lord Jesus Christ.
Through my faith in Him as my Savior, who gave His life
in my place, forgive me of my sins. Give to me the as-
surance that Thou dost love me and make me aware of Thy
presence by my side to protect me and to keep and to help
me throughout eternity. Amen."

28.01

Catholic Act of Contrition (whispered either to or with soldier.

"O my God, I am heartily sorry for having offended Thee and I detest all my sins, because I dread the loss of heaven and the pains of hell, but most of all because they offend Thee, my God, Who art all good and deserving of all my love. I firmly resolve, with the help of Thy grace, to confess my sins, do penance, and to amend my life. Amen."

Prayer for Jewish Personnel

"The soul which Thou, O God, hast given unto me came pure from Thee. Thou hast created it, Thou has formed it and Thou hast breathed it into me. While the breath of life is within me, I will worship Thee, Sovereign of the World, in Whose hands are the souls of all living and the spirits of all flesh.
    Sh'ma Yisroayl, Adonoi Elohaynu,
    Adonoi Echod.
    Hear, O Israel: The Lord our God,
    the Lord is One.
    Boruch shaym K'vod malchuso l'olom
    voed.
    Praised be His name, Whose glorious
    kingdom is for ever and ever.
    V'ohavte ays Adonoi, Elohecho, b'chol
    l'vovcho, u'v'chol naf'sh'cho,
    u'v'chol m'odecho.
    Thou shalt love the Lord, thy God
    with all thy heart, with all thy
    soul and with all thy might."

28.02

CHAPTER TWENTY-NINE

PREPARATION OF A RANGER
TRAINING EXERCISE

1. Carefully analyze written or verbal directive for planning guidance.
   - a. Purpose of exercise.
   - b. Type of training to be stressed.
   - c. Time and place of exercise.
   - d. Units participating.
   - e. Terrain available.
   - f. Ammunition and special equipment.
   - g. Other guidance commander desires to give.

2. Conduct a research of all tactical and administrative references pertaining to Ranger training. (FM 21-75, FM 21-50)
   - a. Tactical references:
     - (1) Field manuals.
     - (2) Training films.
     - (3) Service school publications.
     - (4) Training circulars and training bulletins.
     - (5) S3 files of previously conducted or similar exercises.
   - b. Administrative references.
     - (1) Unit SOP.
     - (2) Garrison regulations.
     - (3) Safety regulations.
     - (4) Army regulations.

3. Make a map reconnaissance and a ground reconnaissance in order to formulate a tentative plan.
   - a. Study the terrain assigned to you on the map.
     - (1) Determine the capabilities and limitations of the terrain.

29.01

          (2) Visualize various ways in which the prob
lem may be conducted.

          (3) Use backward planning.

          (4) Tentatively organize the exercise area.

          (5) Plan your ground reconnaissance.

      b. Actually make your ground reconnaissance.

          (1) Start your objective.

          (2) Analyze the terrain.

          (3) Use tentative map plan and walk over
ground.

          (4) Plan your method of control.

          (5) Consider safety limitations.

          (6) Place on map the final plan of action.

          (7) Place on map control elements.

4. Write the problem or scenario.

    a. General situation.

    b. Initial situation or briefing.

    c. Subsequent situations.

    d. Time schedule.

5. Formulate the control plan.

    a. Control elements:

        (1) Principal Instructor.

        (2) Assistant Principal Instructor(s).

        (3) Observer-Instructor.

        (4) Aggressor Control Officer.

        (5) Cadre.

    b. Support elements:

        (1) Friendly troops.

        (2) Aggressor troops.

        (3) Transportation.

        (4) Medics.

        (5) Communication.

        (6) Supply.

        (7) Others.

    c. Evacuation plan.

29.02

6. Effect administrative coordination for personnel, equipment, transportation, etc.

7. Prepare terrain in exercise area per scenario.

8. Brief cadre, support and Aggressor personnel.

9. Conduct rehearsals. (Critique thoroughly through out.)

10. Conduct exercise.

11. Critique student action.

12. Write after-action report (if required).

CHAPTER THIRTY

CONFIDENCE TESTS

1. OBJECTIVE: To increase the confidence of soldiers by requiring them to negotiate obstacles which appear more difficult than they actually are.

2. SUSPENSION TRAVERSE (See figure 1):
    a. Execution: The student climbs a pole or tree by the use of a rope ladder or spikes. Places a pulley on the steel cable and slides down and drops into the water on command.
    b. Reference: TM 21-200, FM 21-50.

3. ROPE DROP CONFIDENCE TEST (See figure 2):
    a. Execution: The student starts at point A, climbs a vertical pole to point B, by the use of metal spikes, walks log to point C, crosses point C without the use of his hands and moves to point D, climbs the knotted rope to point E, monkey crawls the horizontal rope to point F, grips the rope with his hands, lowers his feet, and, on command, drops into the water.
    b. References: TM 21-200, FM 21-50.

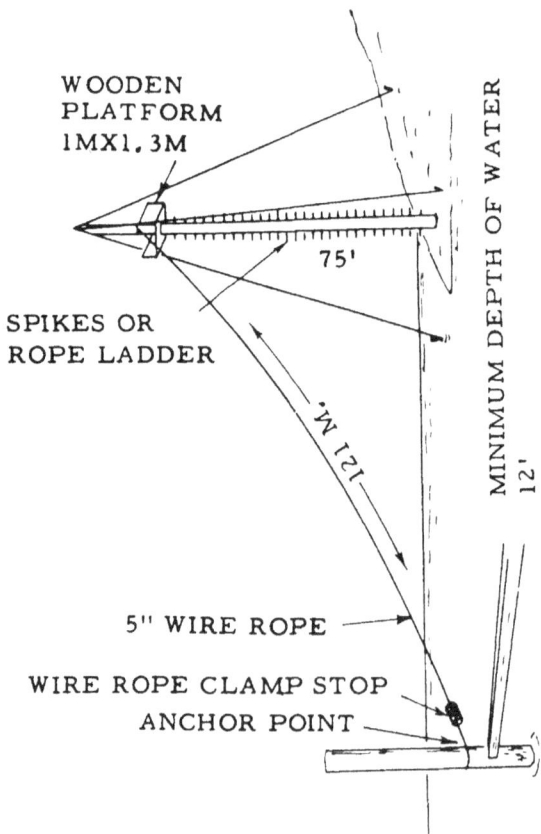

WOODEN
PLATFORM
1MX1.3M

SPIKES OR
ROPE LADDER

75'

121 M.

MINIMUM DEPTH OF WATER

12'

5" WIRE ROPE

WIRE ROPE CLAMP STOP
ANCHOR POINT

Figure 1. Suspension Traverse.

30.02

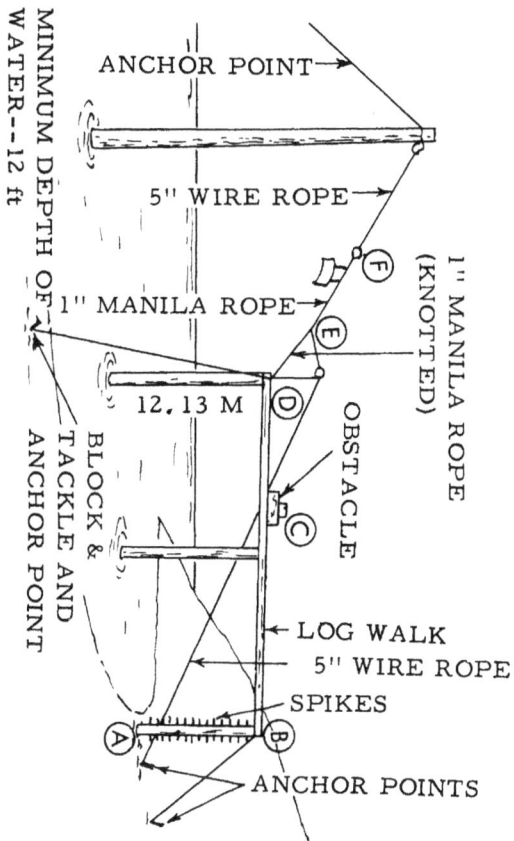

Figure 2. Rope Drop.

30.03

CHAPTER THIRTY-ONE

NAVIGATION TRAINING

PART ONE - Distance Determination

1. OBJECTIVE: To enable the student to become proficient in distance determination through pacing over a measured course.

    a. The student must be able to determine ground distance over varied terrain by means of pacing.

    b. The soldier's pace count for each 100 meters of ground distance will fluctuate as he encounters varied types of terrain.

    c. A pace that is to be used over varied terrain must be acquired from walking over such terrain to be reliable. Any pace, to be reliable, should be checked over a distance of at least 600 meters.

2. SAMPLE LAYOUT - See next page.

31.01

Sample Layout

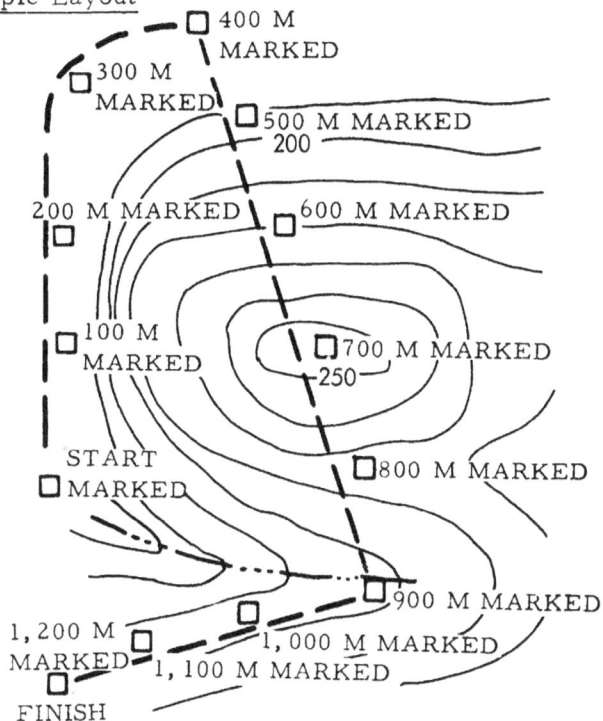

PART TWO - Mechanical Compass Course

1. OBJECTIVE: Make an individual aware of his
tendencies to drift or bear right or left while following a
given azimuth; instill confidence in his ability and his
equipment, and provide practical work with the compass
in conjunction with pacing.

      a. Nomenclature of Compass:

         (1) Cover.

            (a) Sighting wire.

            (b) Luminous dots.

            (c) Scale.

31. 02

(2) Case.
    (a) Thumb loop.
    (b) Eye piece, lens and sighting slot.
    (c) Bezel ring - rotating outer glass with long and short luminous lines inscribed.
    (d) Black index line or stationary inner glass.
    (e) Floating dial indicator.
  b. Use of the compass.
    (1) Night setting.
      (a) Place desired azimuth under black index line. Rotate bezel ring until long luminous line is directly over north arrow. Follow the long axis of the compass. For rapid movement, use this system both in daylight and in darkness.
    (2) Setting compass using "click" system. Determine the difference in degrees between present and desired azimuth, divide by 3 to determine number of clicks. If desired azimuth is less than present azimuth, rotate bezel ring to the right; if greater, rotate to the left. The proper direction can be remembered by applying the "LARS" rule, which is Left Add, Right Subtract.
  c. Course diagram.
    (1) Each rectangle will train 100 trainees at one time.
    (2) Each rectangle is 180 meters long and 140 meters wide.
    (3) 32 stakes, 20 meters apart around the perimeter of each rectangle. Number of stakes clockwise Make them visible only at a short distance.
    (4) Determine magnetic azimuths between stakes. Establish 5 "leg" course or each trainee.
    (5) Make instruction cards for trainee to use.

31.03

COURSE DIAGRAM

NOTE: Position sufficient cadre around perimeter to correct each trainee after each leg.

    d. Sample Instruction Card:

INSTRUCTION CARD

1. From your present position move on an
   Az 106° for 130 mtrs   (Stake #4)

2. Continue on Az 149° for 85m   (Stake #18)

3. Continue on Az 320° for 106m   (Stake #23)

4. Continue on Az 148° for 200m   (Stake #16)

5. Continue on Az 243° for 130m   (Stake #29)

31.04

PART THREE - Day and Night Compass Course

1. OBJECTIVE: To test the individual soldier's proficiency in day and night compass navigation by a timed, graded, practical exercise.

2. LEVEL OF TRAINING: The soldier must have had training in pacing, fundamentals of map reading, use of compass and terrain association prior to negotiating this test. The soldier should also have run the mechanical compass course.

3. TERRAIN AND MATERIEL:
   a. To accommodate 200 participants without congestion, the training area for the course should be approximately four thousand meters by four thousand meters. This area should include varied terrain with sufficient road nets for control and safety purposes. However, roads and trails should not be used by participants, except for emergencies.
   b. To set up the stakes on the course, you should locate the positions on the map, plot the coordinates and number the positions. For a 200 man group, 21 stakes are sufficient. Locate the positions far enough apart so the individual negotiating the course can't confuse one stake for another. As a guide, the stakes should be at least 400 meters apart.
   c. For control and grading purposes, use different colored routes to the various stakes so that the participant's progress can be easily followed. There may be as many as four colored routes passing through any given numbered stake.
   d. Determine the magnetic azimuths and distances along these colored routes and place this information on a card with the stake number and color route to be followed.
   e. At some of the stakes throughout the course, a map may be provided with an instruction card giving the

31.05

present location by coordinates and a coordinate of the
next stake to be located. This will require the participant
to plot his own route.

      f. There should be more stakes along each
colored route than is required for completion of the test.
This is done so the participant doesn't finish the test on
the same stake from which he started.

      g. Five different colored routes are sufficient to
accommodate 200 participants. If more colored routes
are used, the number of stakes and the size of the training
area should be increased accordingly.

      h. Recommended material to be used for the
stakes are as follows:

      (1) 50 caliber ammunition boxes. These are
excellent in that they may be closed to keep the instruc-
tional material dry.

      (2) Metal piping about two inches in diameter
and about six feet long. This will support the ammunition
box about five feet above the ground, and is durable.

      (3) Both the pipe and the box should be painted
white for easy identification at night.

      (4) The stake number is painted on the side of
the box for identification purposes.

      (5) An area at least 25 meters in diameter
should be cleared around each stake to prevent it from being hidden by heavy brush.

      4. ORGANIZATION: The participants are broken
down into two-man groups, informed of the color route
they will follow and taken to a starting stake. It may be
necessary to have more than one two-man group leaving
from the same stake on the same colored route. Plan so
that they arrive at the starting stake at different times.
This will reduce the possibility of their working together.
The test may also be run as an individual test. In this case
it will be necessary to run each of the colored routes in both

directions, thereby doubling the number of available routes.

5. SCHEDULING: The course should be scheduled so that one-half the practical work is during daylight hours and one-half at night. Consider time needed for briefings and moving the participants to the starting stakes.

6. CONTROL AND SAFETY: Have control vehicles moving through the test area to control, critique and give assistance when needed, as well as for medical evacuation.

7. EVALUATION OF PARTICIPANTS: To grade the test, make a sequence list of the stakes on each colored route. Make all routes go in one direction, either clockwise or counter-clockwise. This will make the sequence of stakes easy to follow. If the participant has the required number of stakes in sequence, he has successfully completed the course. If he is out of sequence on one stake, he does not get credit for that stake but does get credit for the following stakes if they are in sequence.

8. COMPASS COURSE LAYOUT. See next page.

Explanation: Shows 2-route layout, 10 stakes possible on each route. Participants try to achieve 8 stakes in time frame; 6 is passing. Note that same stake boxes are used for both routes at some points to reduce the number of stake boxes needed.

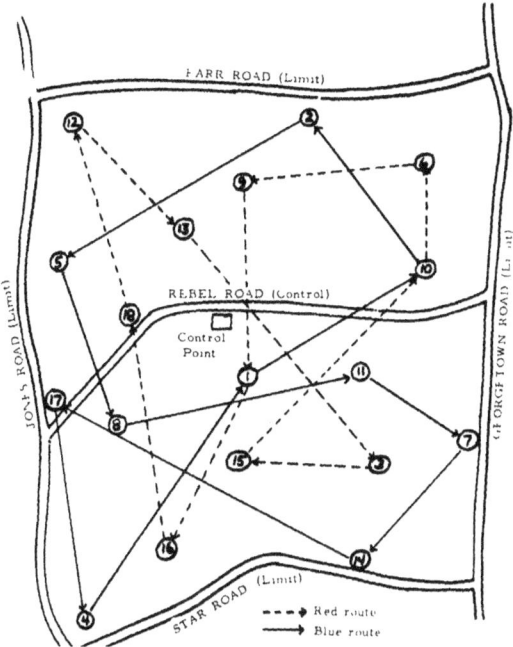

31.08

CHAPTER THIRTY-TWO

COMBAT WATER SURVIVAL

1. PURPOSE. To prepare an individual to encounter water hazards under tactical conditions.

2. GENERAL. All personnel should be able to swim prior to receiving this instruction. Three hours is required to give this class to an 180-man group. A 20-minute presentation should be given initially to acquaint all personnel with the techniques of combat water survival and the method of conducting the test. During this orientation, conservation of strength, breathing techniques, mental control, and preparation of clothing and equipment for operations around water should be stressed. A practical exercise is conducted during the final 2 1/2 hours of instruction.

3. ORGANIZATION.
   a. A swimming pool is organized into four stations
      Station #1--Harness Removal
      Station #2--15-meter Swim with Equipment
      Station #3--Unexpected Entry into Water from
                 a Height
      Station #4--Retest
   b. Stations are progressive and should be taken in numbered order. Each station can effectively handle a squad at a time.
   c. Personnel required for his class are: one principal instructor, 2 assistant instructors for each station, one senior lifeguard for each station.

4. SAFETY. Medical personnel and evacuation means should be available where the class is given. Necessary life-saving equipment, shepherd's crooks, ring buoys should be available at each station.

32.01

5. EVALUATION. At station #4, anyone that fails one or more stations is retested to determine if he is a water risk. Based upon performance in the test and retest if necessary, individuals are placed into one of three categories:

> Water Risk
> Weak Swimmer
> Adequate

Personnel placed in the "water risk" category should be given additional swimming instruction emphasizing the side stroke and the scissors kick.

* 9 7 8 1 5 8 9 6 3 7 9 7 9 *